Wordsworth's Poem of the Mind

an essay on
The Prelude

for
ALICE

Wordsworth's Poem of the Mind

an essay on
The Prelude

RONALD GASKELL

EDINBURGH UNIVERSITY PRESS

© Ronald Gaskell 1991

Edinburgh University Press
22 George Square, Edinburgh

Set in Linotron Palatino
by Photoprint, Torquay, and
printed in Great Britain by
Redwood Press Limited
Melksham, Wiltshire

British Library Cataloguing
in Publication Data

Gaskell, Ronald
   Wordsworth's poem of the mind: an essay on the 'Prelude'.
   1. Poetry in English. Wordsworth, William, 1770–1850
   I. Title
821.7

ISBN 0 7486 0263 1

Contents

Preface

The Prelude is one of the great voyages of discovery, not just a first-hand account (thought it is that too, and an incomparably vivid one) of the boyhood and coming of age of a great poet.

The poems of Wordsworth that most of us value were all written within ten years. Apart from *The Prelude* they are not very numerous – thirty or forty, perhaps. Many of these, including 'Tintern Abbey' and 'Michael', appeared in the first (1798) or second (1800) edition of *Lyrical Ballads*. 'The Ruined Cottage' and its companion piece, 'The Pedlar', were drafted in 1797/98, though not published till their inclusion, considerably revised, in Book I of *The Excursion*. 'Resolution and Independence' belongs to 1802, the 'Ode: Intimations of Immortality' and a few other pieces – 'I wandered lonely as a cloud', 'Stepping Westward', 'The Solitary Reaper', 'Peele Castle' – to the years 1802/6. *The Prelude* itself, begun in 1798, was finished in May 1805, though revised at various times before its publication, a few months after Wordsworth's death, in 1850.

The crucial years, then, the years of Wordsworth's strength as a poet, are from 1797 to 1806. The key text for an understanding of his poetry is *The Prelude*, especially in its two-part (1799) form and in the first complete version of 1805.

The Prelude traces the growth of a poet's mind. This growth was neither simple nor straightforward, and though the poem can be read as a spiritual autobiography, it is clearly a great deal more. I have isolated what I take to be Wordsworth's major concerns: nature and the One Life within us and abroad, the mind's relationship with the world, and the imagination. To treat these separately is doubtless to simplify, for in the poem they overlap and interact. The reason for this, I think, is that at the centre of all three concerns (as of 'Tintern Abbey', which raises the first two) is Wordsworth's conviction of the unique value of feeling. It would only be a slight exaggeration to say that for Wordsworth, while he was writing *The Prelude*, feeling, the mind and the imagination, were three words for the same creative power. The three chapters of this book, therefore, flow into each other, and are divided only in the hope of making Wordsworth's thinking clearer.

That *The Prelude* raises other issues than those I discuss goes without saying. I have not tried to deal with every aspect of the poem, only with those which seem to me central.

Any study of this kind owes a large debt to others. I have found most useful Herbert Lindenberger's *On Wordsworth's 'Prelude'* (Princeton, 1963) and two general books on Wordsworth: John Jones's *The Egotistical Sublime* (1954) and David Ferry's *The Limits of Mortality* (Middletown, Conn., 1959). Jonathan Wordsworth's *The Music of Humanity* (1969) was very helpful on 'The Pedlar' and the One Life.

De Selincourt's great edition of *The Prelude* established the 1805 and 1850 texts, and his Introduction and Notes, revised by Helen Darbishire, are still valuable. More recently the Norton *Prelude*, edited by Jonathan Wordsworth, M. H. Abrams and Stephen Gill, has printed all three versions of the poem. My debt to that edition (from which I quote) is considerable, and I am grateful; without it, indeed, this essay could hardly have been written.

Wordsworth enlarged his Preface to *Lyrical Ballads* for the edition of 1802, and when quoting from the Preface I have used that revised text. References to *The Prelude*, unless otherwise stated, are to the 1805 version.

1

Nature and the One Life

Therefore am I still
A lover of the meadows and the woods
And mountains; and of all that we behold
From this green earth.

'Tintern Abbey'

Wonder not
If such my transports were, for in all things
I saw one life, and felt that it was joy.

The Prelude II.428

'Tintern Abbey' found itself in the first edition of *Lyrical Ballads* (1798) almost by accident. The collection Wordsworth and Coleridge had put together was already with the printer when Dorothy and her brother set off in July for their walking tour of the Wye valley. They returned to Bristol a few days later, Wordsworth finishing the poem on the way. Apparently he was still finishing it as they walked down Park Street, and went straight to Cottle's shop to write it out. In print it sits a little oddly alongside poems like 'The Thorn' and 'The Idiot Boy', but the title page, *Lyrical Ballads with a Few Other Poems*, already covered the 'Yew-tree' lines and Coleridge's 'Nightingale', and 'Tintern Abbey' brings the book to an impressive close.

The genre to which its first readers would relate it, the poetry of landscape and moral generalisation, was well established. For Wordsworth, as for Thomson and Cowper, woods and streams lead naturally to reflections on human life. But for Wordsworth this means primarily his own life, especially the life of feeling, where to reflect is also to clarify and evaluate. This is not a process of analysis and deduction. It is a matter of keeping open to experience; of listening to the heart and allowing its promptings to remind us how the present keeps faith with the past; of renewing the conscious mind from the hidden sources of its strength, and so confirming the values that will steady it through the future. My opinion, said Coleridge in a letter to Poole of 23 March 1801, is this: 'that deep thinking is attainable only by a man of deep feeling, and that all truth is a species of revelation.' Wordsworth would have agreed with the first proposition, and perhaps also with the second.

'Tintern Abbey' was the last poem Wordsworth wrote before sailing for Germany with Dorothy and Coleridge in September 1798 – the last poem, therefore, before the child-hood episodes of *The Prelude* were drafted that winter. In many ways it anticipates the longer poem. Syntax and metre are handled with the same confidence, the same fidelity to thought and feeling, as the mind moves back and forward in time between the present and the past. But the connection goes deeper. Like *The Prelude*, 'Tintern Abbey' raises awkward questions in psychology and metaphysics. And like *The Prelude*, 'Tintern Abbey' makes it clear that, except for a brief period, Wordsworth's feeling for nature – 'The guide, the guardian of my heart, and soul / Of all my moral being' – was never simply or even mainly a delight of the senses. The point is worth establishing in detail.

I

The opening of 'Tintern Abbey', with its qualifications and quiet distinctions, sets the mood for the first fifty lines or so of the poem. Wordsworth seems to be thinking his way forward, the verse has the air of being improvised, yet rhythm and syntax register every nuance of feeling:

> Five years have passed; five summers, with the length
> Of five long winters! and again I hear
> These waters, rolling from their mountain-springs
> With a soft inland murmur. – Once again
> Do I behold these steep and lofty cliffs,
> That on a wild secluded scene impress
> Thoughts of more deep seclusion; and connect
> The landscape with the quiet of the sky.
> The day is come when I again repose
> Here, under this dark sycamore, and view
> These plots of cottage-ground, these orchard-tufts,

Which at this season, with their unripe fruits,
Are clad in one green hue, and lose themselves
'Mid groves and copses. Once again I see
These hedge-rows, hardly hedge-rows, little lines
Of sportive wood run wild: these pastoral farms,
Green to the very door; and wreaths of smoke
Sent up, in silence, from among the trees!

Wordsworth first saw the Wye valley in the summer of 1793, not long after his return from France. It was a time of tension and distress in his personal life. Separated from Annette and their newborn child (Caroline was born in December 1792), he had no home and no profession of any kind. In *The Prelude* he speaks more than once of that summer – of the Isle of Wight, where each evening for a month he heard the ominous sound of the cannon at sunset as the British fleet waited to sail against France, and of the dreary wastes of Salisbury Plain that gave birth to the poem which finally became 'Guilt and Sorrow'. Between then and his second visit to the Wye in 1798 lay the long moral and spiritual crisis he explores in Books X–XII of *The Prelude*: the collapse of his youthful faith in the Revolution, the struggle to find some ground in reason or the heart on which to build his hopes for mankind, and the gradual recovery, with Dorothy's affection and the friendship of Coleridge to sustain him, of his confidence in his own powers and direction as a poet.

All this lies behind, and gives weight to, the reflections wakened by the murmur of the river and the secluded landscape that so often has brought him not only 'tranquil restoration', but 'that serene and blessed mood' in which

with an eye made quiet by the power
Of harmony and the deep power of joy
We see into the life of things.

Perhaps (there are few certainties in 'Tintern Abbey') this is a vain belief. Yet

How oft in spirit have I turned to thee,
O sylvan Wye! thou wanderer through the woods,
How often has my spirit turned to thee!

With the next paragraph the feeling grows more complex. Perplexed by the change between the scene as he remembered it, from his visit five years earlier, and the wooded cliffs he again sees before him, Wordsworth recognises a deeper change in himself. And recognising this change he tries, almost for the first time, to understand the development of his feeling for nature.

His childhood, rather surprisingly, is dismissed in a parenthesis – '(The coarser pleasures of my boyish days / And their glad animal movements all gone by)' – for the contrast Wordsworth is struck by is not between the man he has become and the boy of twenty years ago, but between 1798 and 1793.

At that first encounter with the Wye, when he was twenty-three, his feeling for nature had been eager, even vehement:

> I cannot paint
> What then I was. The sounding cataract
> Haunted me like a passion: the tall rock,
> The mountain, and the deep and gloomy wood,
> Their colours and their forms, were then to me
> An appetite; a feeling and a love,
> That had no need of a remoter charm,
> By thought supplied, nor any interest
> Unborrowed from the eye. – That time is past,
> And all its aching joys are now no more,
> And all its dizzy raptures.

His response on that first visit had been passionately sensuous. And we can link this with his reference in *The Prelude* to the same period, when nature offered itself as an escape from the moral and intellectual anguish of Salisbury Plain, the separation from Annette, and the British declaration of war on the French republic. In Book XI (of the 1805 *Prelude*) Wordsworth speaks of the relief of that return to nature in 1793 as violent but superficial: a time when the eye, 'the most despotic of our senses' (XI.173), was master of the heart:

> Here only let me add that my delights,
> Such as they were, were sought insatiably.

Though 'twas a transport of the outward sense,
Not of the mind – vivid but not profound –
Yet was I often greedy in the chace,
And roamed from hill to hill, from rock to rock,
Still craving combinations of new forms,
New pleasure, wider empire for the sight,
Proud of its own endowments, and rejoiced
To lay the inner faculties asleep.   (XI.185)

This 'degradation', as he calls it, was transient. As a boy he had loved nature more deeply, not only rejoicing in 'the winds / And powerful waters' (XI.140) but responding to them with his whole heart. And this deep love he had carried with him, he tells us, as late as his walking tour through the Alps in the summer of 1790.

The sensuous transports of 1793, then, were an aberration:

I had felt
Too forcibly, too early in my life,
Visitings of imaginative power
For this to last: I shook the habit off
Entirely and for ever, and again
In Nature's presence stood, as I stand now,
A sensitive, and a *creative* soul.   (XI.250)

The self of 1793 is judged, and judged to be unworthy. But these passages I have been quoting from *The Prelude* were drafted early in 1805, nearly a dozen years after the period they refer to, as part of Wordsworth's account of how his imagination had been 'impaired' on his return from France. The sensuous excitements of 1793, he now felt, were both a symptom and a contributory cause of that impairment. He is much harder, therefore, in *The Prelude* on the young man who first visited the Wye valley that summer than he had wanted to be when he went back there in 1798.

True, the comparable lines in 'Tintern Abbey' hint at a feeling for nature on his first visit that was anything but spiritual. The sounding cataract 'haunted me like a passion'. Wood and mountain, their forms and colours, were 'an appetite'. Yet the joys and raptures of that time are recalled in 'Tintern Abbey' with a deep sense of loss. Their memory,

after all, had brought moments of restoration, had led him
even to 'that serene and blessed mood' in which we see into
the life of things. And when he turns, as he does towards the
close of the poem, to his beloved sister, catching in her voice
'the language of my former heart', it is to hope that for a little
longer he may see in her 'what I was once'.

As often in Wordsworth, we have two quite different
perspectives: 1793 seen from 1798 ('Tintern Abbey'), and 1793
seen from 1805 (*Prelude* XI). The two are not incompatible,
but the second judges the younger self more harshly.

II

From the review of his earlier self and its passions Wordsworth
moves in 'Tintern Abbey' to the theme that will carry his
poem to a subdued climax. In the years since his first visit he
has learned to look at nature with a full recognition of the
sadness of human life:

> And I have felt
> A presence that disturbs me with the joy
> Of elevated thoughts; a sense sublime
> Of something far more deeply interfused,
> Whose dwelling is the light of setting suns,
> And the round ocean and the living air,
> And the blue sky, and in the mind of man:
> A motion and a spirit, that impels
> All thinking things, all objects of all thought,
> And rolls through all things.

Whether any logical ground could be adduced for the belief
in a presence that has its dwelling in 'the round ocean and
the living air' no less than in the mind of man, we are not
encouraged to ask. What we are told, what the poetry proves,
is that Wordsworth has felt it. And the music of the verse
guides us through to the end of the paragraph:

> Therefore am I still
> A lover of the meadows and the woods,
> And mountains; and of all that we behold
> From this green earth; of all the mighty world
> Of eye, and ear, – both what they half create,

> And what perceive; well pleased to recognise
> In nature and the language of the sense,
> The anchor of my purest thoughts, the nurse,
> The guide, the guardian of my heart, and soul
> Of all my moral being.

This is more complex than it looks at first. To relate the mystical experience of 'something far more deeply interfused' to 'nature and the language of the sense' is not easy. And to complicate matters further, Wordsworth goes out of his way to remind us that 'this green earth' is not just given to the senses. We 'half create' it.

For the first edition of *Lyrical Ballads* Wordsworth added a note on this phrase, referring his readers to a line in Young, 'the exact expression of which I cannot recollect'. If we look up the relevant passage in *Night Thoughts* (vi.413–27), we find that Young was referring to what Locke called the secondary qualities of things – colour, smell, taste, sound, texture; the primary qualities (squareness, weight, etc.) are those that can be measured. Is this the distinction Wordsworth had in mind? Perhaps. Or again, since his recollection of Young was a little hazy, perhaps not. At all events, if we half create the world of the senses, may it not be that we also half create, or even wholly create, the 'presence' that has its dwelling in the living air and the blue sky? Wordsworth does not ask himself this, though the possibility had occurred to him a few months earlier when he was writing 'The Pedlar'. But if we pause for a moment, as the paragraphing of 'Tintern Abbey' allows us to, we find ourselves with two very puzzling questions:

1) is nature animated by a divine energy, or is that energy simply a projection of the human mind?

2) how far do we, does each of us, create the world that we perceive?

There is no simple answer to either of these questions. Wordsworth himself was not clear about them, and offers different, sometimes contradictory, answers at different times. (*The Prelude*, it is important to remember, was composed over a period of seven years. What Wordsworth thought in 1805 is not always what he thought in 1798.) Any discussion of his poetry has to tackle both questions, and of course they are intimately related. The first, which I want to take up in a moment, Wordsworth had already broached in 'The Pedlar' (Jan./March 1798). The second, which we will come to in the next chapter, raises a further issue: the validity of the poetic imagination in its dealings with the world. In *The Prelude* all three topics get involved with each other – in a sense they form a single problem – so that a reader of the poem occasionally finds himself going round in circles. It will be convenient, however, to treat them separately and to begin with the religious/metaphysical question: is there, as Wordsworth was ready to claim in 1798, a motion and a spirit that 'rolls through all things'?

Before Wordsworth had given much thought to this, the question had troubled Coleridge. Prominent in Coleridge's early poetry is a strong religious impulse, never quite integrated with his keen sensibility to form and colour, light and shade, in nature. In several poems of 1794–97 – 'Religious Musings', 'The Eolian Harp', 'The Destiny of Nations' and or two others – this religious impulse finds expression as an enthusiastic if speculative pantheism. Coleridge at the time (he was not yet twenty-five) was deeply impressed by the Unitarian Joseph Priestley, who held that the universe is permeated by a kind of spiritual energy. He had also been reading Spinoza, the seventeenth-century mystic Jacob Boehme, and the English Neoplatonists of the seventeenth century. Coleridge's problem was to reconcile their ideas with his Christian faith, since pantheism, which identifies nature with God, is incompatible with a religion of transcendence.

In 'The Eolian Harp' (1795, but improved the following year) Coleridge wonders:

> And what if all of animated nature
> Be but organic harps diversely framed
> That tremble into thought, as o'er them sweeps
> Plastic and vast, one intellectual breeze,
> At once the soul of each and God of all?

'Plastic', as always with Coleridge, means shaping, giving form to something inchoate, and 'intellectual' here has a sense very close to 'spiritual'. But the thrust of Coleridge's question is not quite clear. Is it only 'animated nature' that is swept by the intellectual/spiritual breeze (an Eolian harp is a lyre that can be played by the wind), while rocks and stones remain obstinately inert? More probably he means that the whole universe is animated.[1] Coleridge, in other words, is struggling to unify – or rather to see as in reality unified – three realms we usually think of as discontinuous: the inorganic world of rocks and stones, the organic world of plant and animal, and the world of mind or spirit.

Language, which codifies our normal habits of thinking and perception, resists any attempt to get beyond these habits. Something can be done by suggestion, especially rhythm, rather than statement; something, too, by metaphor (the wind harps 'tremble into thought'). Or one or two words can be stretched a little, the resulting imprecision being accepted for the sake of what could not otherwise be said. The difficulty for the reader, especially with this last resource, is how to distinguish fresh insight, a pushing forward of the frontiers of perception, from a well-meant semantic haze. In 'The Destiny of Nations' (1796) God is addressed as 'Nature's vast ever-acting energy! / In will, in deed, impulse of all to all!' which anticipates, in a slightly different key, Wordsworth's sense of 'A motion and a spirit that impels / All thinking things, all objects of all thought' in 'Tintern Abbey'. Energy seems to be a useful concept if we are trying, as Coleridge was trying, to bridge the gap between spirit and the material world. But will the bridge take much weight? (One end looks a good deal stronger than the other.)

Again, in a late addition to 'The Eolian Harp', Coleridge cries:

> O! the one Life within us and abroad
> Which meets all motion and becomes its soul,
> A light in sound, a sound-like power in light,
> Rhythm in all thought, and joyance everywhere.

In its context this reads persuasively. The trouble with any discussion of it, or of similar passages in Wordsworth, is that the word 'life' is never defined, and perhaps cannot be. In the ordinary way we think of it as marking off the organic, the world of growth and reproduction, from the inorganic. Birds and trees are alive; rocks, streams and clouds are not.

This is a real distinction, not one 'which we have made' (*Prelude* II.224), and why we should elide it, much as we might like to, is not clear. Nor can we save the appearances by leaving rocks and streams to one side. For suppose we do: how then does the one Life within us and abroad, as we respond to it in tree and bird, differ from the vitality which (no one has ever disputed) links us in sympathy with all living things?

I raise these questions not with any thought of going into them in detail, but to suggest the complexity of the issues Wordsworth touches on in 'Tintern Abbey' and explores, or occasionally sidesteps, in *The Prelude*. Wordsworth in 1798 was not in any sense that matters a Christian, but from Platonism and Christianity he had inherited, as we still inherit, a dualistic view of the universe. In this view nature and man are both amphibians, living at once in a realm of spirit and a world of matter. No philosophic position is easier to criticise. Most of us nevertheless make do with it, or some variant of it, as Wordsworth did, if only because the alternatives seem even less believable and less attractive. Materialism cannot account for consciousness and eliminates the freedom of the will. Idealism reduces the body to a prison and the world to a play of shadows. If we reject both these alternatives we are left with the questions Wordsworth and Coleridge were struggling to resolve: what is the relation between the visible world and the invisible, the world of mind or spirit? Is there a divine mind, wholly transcendent, immanent, or both? If immanent, how does spirit permeate the stubborn materiality of the world? And is the human mind or spirit a fragment of the divine?

How much Wordsworth's thinking about these questions was prompted or deepened by Coleridge can only be conjecture. When 'The Eolian Harp' and 'The Destiny of Nations' were written, in 1795/96, the two poets scarcely knew each other. But ideas of nature, the physical universe, as animated by spirit or energy seem to have been in the air. Wordsworth, when he was altering his copy of *An Evening Walk* in April 1794, claims something of the kind in a few couplets which he never published:

A heart that vibrates evermore, awake
To feeling for all forms that Life can take,
That wider still its sympathies extends
And sees not any line where being ends;
Sees sense, through Nature's rudest forms betrayed,
Tremble obscure in fountain, rock and shade,
And while a secret power those forms endears,
Their social accents never vainly hears.[2]

At the same time, an idea is not an emotion. Coleridge's delight in nature was genuine, but his mind had a more philosophical bias, a deeper need for an intellectually coherent account of experience, than Wordsworth's. It was Coleridge who gave us the phrase 'the one Life within us and abroad'. It is 'Tintern Abbey' and *The Prelude*, rather than any poem of Coleridge's, that give that life its most passionate expression.

III

In *The Prelude* the One Life is affirmed (and questioned) in a splendid passage, adapted from 'The Pedlar', in Book II. Long before we reach that passage, however, we have been alerted by a number of suggestions to the possibility that nature has a life akin to ours – a life of feeling, even perhaps of consciousness. These suggestions, each one slight but cumulatively telling, are not deliberate. They are there because for a while they were part of Wordsworth's vision of the world. Often they amount to nothing more than the overtones of a verb, as when he recalls 'the calm / Which Nature breathes among the hills and groves' (I.284). The opening of Book I is characteristic:

Oh there is blessing in this gentle breeze
That blows from the green fields and from the clouds
And from the sky; it beats against my cheek
And seems half conscious of the joy it gives.   (I.1)

The joy is transient, an emotion of the moment. But just for that reason, because the lines read so impulsively, we are drawn into Wordsworth's feelings. There is 'blessing', not just pleasure, in the breeze, and it blows not only from the green fields but from the clouds and from the sky, as if the whole vale encompassed the poet in its blessing. Is the breeze conscious, then, of the joy it brings? Apparently not. Yet it seems *half* conscious.[3] So the impression, however faint, we carry forward as we read on is one of nature as in some way happily alive.

The impression is strengthened by the first great wave of feeling in the poem:

> Was it for this
> That one, the fairest of all rivers, loved
> To blend his murmurs with my nurse's song,
> And from his alder shades and rocky falls,
> And from his fords and shallows, sent a voice
> That flowed along my dreams? For this didst thou,
> O Derwent, travelling over the green plains
> Near my 'sweet birthplace', didst thou, beauteous stream,
> Make ceaseless music through the night and day,
> Which with its steady cadence, tempering
> Our human waywardness, composed my thoughts
> To more than infant softness, giving me
> Among the fretful dwellings of mankind
> A knowledge, a dim earnest, of the calm
> Which Nature breathes among the hills and groves?   (I.271)

The precision of 'alder shades and rocky falls' is reassuring: there is nothing sentimental about a memory that sees the past as clearly as this. But 'the calm / Which Nature breathes' tells us something else: that the child already had 'a dim earnest' of a larger presence, less definite but not less real than rocks and trees.

For a small boy the river is naturally 'he'. Having left 'his mountains' for the towers of Cockermouth, the Derwent flowed past the end of the garden where Wordsworth (and his brothers) played as a child:

> He was a playmate whom we dearly loved:
> Oh, many a time have I, a five years' child,
> A naked boy, in one delightful rill,
> A little mill-race severed from his stream,

Made one long bathing of a summer's day,
Basked in the sun, and plunged, and basked again,
Alternate, all a summer's day, or coursed
Over the sandy fields, leaping through groves
Of yellow grunsel; or, when, crag and hill,
The woods, and distant Skiddaw's lofty height,
Were bronzed with a deep radiance, stood alone
Beneath the sky, as if I had been born
On Indian plains, and from my mother's hut
Had run abroad in wantonness to sport,
A naked savage, in the thunder-shower.   (I.290)

With a passage like this it is necessary to quote a dozen or twenty lines, for only then does the sweep of syntax and rhythm suggest the strength of feeling that inspired them. At times, however, a single phrase can be significant. In three of the four episodes recounted in Book I – snaring woodcock, climbing for ravens' eggs, the stolen boat on Ullswater – the child has a sense of Nature as a living thing. Not that this is ever directly stated. It is something vaguely felt, occasionally as joy, often as a threat. We hear of 'low breathings coming after me', and of the 'strange utterance' of the wind among the crags. Even at the close of the skating episode, the movement of the earth –

> yet still the solitary cliffs
> Wheeled by me, even as if the earth had rolled
> With visible motion her diurnal round.   (I.484)

– carries a hint of life in the unobtrusive 'her'.

Feelings of this kind are everywhere in Wordsworth's memories of childhood. In Book II the sun, like the Derwent, is remembered with the love that makes personification natural: 'I had seen him lay / His beauty on the morning hills' (II.188); the moon was equally dear:

> For I would dream away my purposes
> Standing to look upon her, while she hung
> Midway between the hills as if she knew
> No other region but belonged to thee,

> Yea, appertained by a peculiar right
> To thee and thy grey huts, my darling vale.   (II.197)

Of course sun and moon and the earth are often personified
even in everyday speech. This is one reason why Wordsworth's poetry is so convincing. The animism latent in most,
perhaps all, languages – though the sun is not always
masculine nor the moon always feminine – lies deep below
the entirely natural 'she hung' (of the moon), 'his mountains'
(of the Derwent) and the strangely powerful 'rolled . . . her
diurnal round'.

It is this kind of animism that links the child with the
primitive; and the poetic imagination has affinities with the
primitive. In the draft of 'Nutting' which Dorothy sent to
Coleridge in a letter of December 1798, Wordsworth speaks
of being led through the wood by guardian spirits –

> They led me far,
> Those guardian spirits, into some dear nook
> Unvisited

– and after he has ravaged the tree,

> the shady nook
> Of hazels, and the green and mossy bower,
> Deformed and sullied, patiently gave up
> Their quiet spirit.

When the poem appeared in print, in the second edition of
Lyrical Ballads (1800), all these spirits had vanished: the first
(the guardian spirits) without trace, the second ('Their quiet
spirit') altered to 'Their quiet being'. The end of the poem,
however, survived unchanged:

> Then, dearest Maiden! move along these shades
> In gentleness of heart; with gentle hand
> Touch – for there is a Spirit in the woods.

The capital in the last line may be the printer's (Dorothy's
transcript of 1798 reads 'spirit'), but the faith is Wordsworth's, and one he was reluctant to give up.

'Nutting' was written at the same time as the boyhood
scenes of *The Prelude*, and in these too Wordsworth's first

drafts are revealing. Book I of the 1805 *Prelude* corresponds roughly to Part I of the 1798/99 MS,[4] but details of phrasing have been altered, sometimes radically. The 'spirits' and 'quiet powers' that guide the child in 1799 (I.67–80) become simply 'Nature' in 1805 (I.362–71). More surprisingly, a passage that in 1799 began

> Ah, not in vain ye beings of the hills,
> And ye that walk the woods and open heaths
> By moon or star-light   (1799, I.130)

reappears in 1805 as:

> Wisdom and spirit of the universe,
> Thou soul that art the eternity of thought . . .   (I.428)

though the 1805 text itself still turns to

> Ye presences of Nature, in the sky
> Or on the earth, ye visions of the hills
> And souls of lonely places,   (I.490)

where the 1799 version of these lines had a more literary colouring.[5]

In one passage of this kind Wordsworth allowed his first draft to stand. But here, as so often in the finest poetry of *The Prelude*, a spiritual awareness barely hinted at is inseparable from the sensuous and emotional life of the child. Wordsworth has been riding with his friends through the ruins of an old chapel:

> Through the walls we flew
> And down the valley, and, a circuit made
> In wantonness of heart, through rough and smooth
> We scampered homeward. Oh, ye rocks and streams,
> And that still spirit of the evening air,
> Even in this joyous time I sometimes felt
> Your presence, when, with slackened step, we breathed
> Along the sides of the steep hills, or when,
> Lighted by gleams of moonlight from the sea,
> We beat with thundering hoofs the level sand.   (II.135)

'Scampered' gives us the excitement of the boy. Then a rush of feeling ('Oh ye rocks and streams') is checked for a

moment – not 'you' or 'thou', but 'that' still spirit of the
evening air – before 'I sometimes felt / Your presence', as the
rhythm gathers strength for the hoofbeats of the final penta-
meter.

IV

Wordsworth is a poet, not a philosopher. This means that his
ability to find words and rhythms for experience is far greater
than his ability to analyse and explain the experience to
himself. Moreover, it is often a delicate matter to distinguish
between what Wordsworth says and what, on the evidence
of the poetry, he really feels. If we believe, or suspend our
disbelief, in the One Life, it is because the poetry carries
conviction. Sometimes in *The Prelude* it does, but not always.
Here is a longer passage from Book I:

> Wisdom and spirit of the universe,
> Thou soul that art the eternity of thought,
> That giv'st to forms and images a breath
> And everlasting motion – not in vain,
> By day or star-light, thus from my first dawn
> Of childhood didst thou intertwine for me
> The passions that build up our human soul,
> Not with the mean and vulgar works of man,
> But with high objects, with enduring things,
> With life and Nature, purifying thus
> The elements of feeling and of thought,
> And sanctifying by such discipline
> Both pain and fear, until we recognise
> A grandeur in the beatings of the heart.   (I.428)

At a casual reading we might take the first few lines for an
echo of 'Tintern Abbey'. When we look more closely, certain
differences grow clear. 'Wisdom' had no place in 'Tintern
Abbey', where Wordsworth was 'disturbed' by the joy of
elevated thoughts. And the soul which gives 'breath / And
everlasting motion' to forms and images sounds less at home
in nature than the spirit that impels and 'rolls through' all
things in the earlier poem. More pervasive, though for that
reason harder to define, is a change of tone. Partly this is a
matter of rhythm. Even more it has to do with the contrast

between the quiet exultation of 'And I have felt . . .' in
'Tintern Abbey' and the direct rhetorical apostrophe of the
Prelude lines. De Selincourt's text, based on Dorothy's MS,
has capitals and a flurry of exclamation marks –

> Wisdom and Spirit of the universe!
> Thou Soul that art the eternity of thought!
> That giv'st to forms and images a breath
> And everlasting motion!

– but even without these the resonance of that opening
sounds a little forced.[6]

No doubt the passage reads more emphatically in isolation
than it does when we are absorbed in the poem. And in any
account of Wordsworth's religion or philosophy of nature it
is important to have as context for the discussion a reminder
of the immediacy and strength of his feelings for the landscape of his boyhood: the Derwent, with its 'alder shades and
rocky falls', and the woods, lakes and mountains around
Hawkshead. In the first two books of *The Prelude* the tributes
to Nature, her 'presences' and her 'overflowing soul', are
rooted in the vivid realism of the skating lines, the episode
of the stolen boat on Ullswater, and the raven's nest on the
crags. Without these even the most impassioned generalis-
ations would mean nothing. But 'Wisdom and spirit of the
universe', with its faintly Christian or Deistic overtones,
comes immediately after the haunting close of the stolen boat
sequence:

> and after I had seen
> That spectacle, for many days my brain
> Worked with a dim and undetermined sense
> Of unknown modes of being. In my thoughts
> There was a darkness – call it solitude
> Or blank desertion – no familiar shapes
> Of hourly objects, images of trees,
> Of sea or sky, no colours of green fields,
> But huge and mighty forms that do not live
> Like living men moved slowly through my mind
> By day, and were the trouble of my dreams.   (I. 417)

The 'Wisdom and spirit of the universe' paragraph, though

it cannot damage these wonderful lines, comes out of the air
with disconcerting abruptness. But then Book I, no less than
the later books of *The Prelude*, emerged after a good deal of
splicing and re-shuffling. The substance of the 'Wisdom and
spirit' paragraph originally followed the raven's nest (not the
stolen boat), and in a form quite different from the text we
have in 1805. In December 1799, though Wordsworth had
moved the paragraph to its present position, it still began like
this:

> Ah, not in vain ye beings of the hills,
> And ye that walk the woods and open heaths
> By moon or star-light, thus from my first dawn
> Of childhood did ye love to intertwine
> The passions that build up our human soul . . .
>   (1799, I.130)

The transformation of these lines into the abstract, even
orthodox, 'Wisdom and spirit of the universe' probably dates
from January 1804 (when Book I took its present shape) and
seems to be one of the earliest signs of that anxiety to avoid
any appearance of pantheism, or nature worship, that would
lead Wordsworth to weaken so many passages between 1805
and 1850.

The line between pantheism and Deism is not always easy
to draw. Deism, however, usually presupposes transcendence and is often thought of as the religion (if that is the
word) of those who saw the universe as a vast machine with
God as the divine mechanic. Wordsworth was as determined
to distance himself from that position as from the charge of
pantheism. In a letter of December 1814 to Catherine Clarkson
he takes to task a friend of hers who (in Wordsworth's view)
had misread his poetry:

> She talks of my being a worshipper of Nature – a
> passionate expression uttered incautiously in the poem
> upon the Wye has led her into this mistake – she reading
> in cold-heartedness and substituting the letter for the
> spirit.

But it is particularly *The Excursion* (just published) that Wordsworth wants to defend:

> She condemns me for not distinguishing between

Nature as the work of God and God himself. But where does she find this doctrine inculcated? Where does she gather that the author of *The Excursion* looks upon Nature and God as the same? He does not indeed consider the supreme Being as bearing the same relation to the Universe as a watch-maker bears to a watch.

The Prelude, of course, had not been published. But *The Prelude* is a very different poem from *The Excursion*, and in the first two books (at any rate in the 1805 version) the distinction between God and Nature is often blurred.

For the Christian this distinction is of some importance. Nature itself is not sacred, though God may be recognised as present in his creation. Addison, long before Wordsworth, observed that: 'Every particle of matter is actuated by this Almighty Being which passes through it. The heavens and the earth, the stars and planets, move and gravitate by virtue of this great principle within them.'[7]

And Thomson, a few years later, asks how Newton, who had seen and understood the order of the whole material universe, could 'Forbear incessant to adore that Power / Who fills, sustains and actuates the whole?'[8] In paraphrase Wordsworth may appear to be saying nothing more than Addison and Thomson, whether we call that Deism or Christianity. The difference, which any reading of *The Prelude* brings out at once, lies in the depth and intensity of Wordsworth's passion for the natural world.

Wordsworth's feeling for nature was certainly religious. It was not always, though it was sometimes, pantheistic. So far as we can reconstruct his development, it seems that the animism of boyhood and later – the spirits (powers, beings, presences) he speaks of in 'Nutting' and the 1799 *Prelude* – merged imperceptibly into a larger awareness, often rapturous, of the One Life. This too was a joy he knew first at Hawkshead. In 'The Pedlar' he assigns it to two different periods ('Ere his ninth year', and 'before his twentieth year was passed'), in *The Prelude* chiefly to his seventeenth year (II.405). In the spring and summer of 1798, when 'The Pedlar' and 'Tintern Abbey' were written, he seems to have recovered, at least intermittently, something of the same joy.

But in *The Prelude* joy is only one element in Wordsworth's spiritual experience. There are others, more elusive and more disquieting: the 'unknown modes of being', for example, which haunt the child's mind after the incident with the stolen boat. There are moods of 'shadowy exultation', hours 'by form or image unprofaned' (II.321–41); moments when the sky 'seemed not a sky / Of earth, and with what motion moved the clouds!' (I.349); moments too, though this is much later,

> when the light of sense
> Goes out in flashes that have shewn to us
> The invisible world.   (VI.534)

If these experiences have anything in common, it is not with intuitions of the One Life but with those 'obstinate questionings / Of sense and outward things' Wordsworth recalls in the 'Immortality Ode'. In a lyric of March 1802, 'To the Cuckoo', the call of the bird – 'No bird but an invisible thing, / A voice, a mystery' – brings Wordsworth a tale of 'visionary hours', when the earth seemed 'insubstantial': not unreal, perhaps, but not the only reality.

Wordsworth's experiences of the numinous, then, seem to have been of two quite different kinds: joy in the One Life and intuitions, glimpses, of a transcendent reality. These two modes of feeling, if translated into concepts, might prove logically so opposed as to be irreconcilable. Wordsworth was not concerned to reconcile them, only to record each experience, however mysterious, in turn. So at any moment in Books I and II of *The Prelude* we can find ourselves, with Wordsworth, moving from one to the other.[9]

For that matter, the One Life itself was never with Wordsworth a coherent structure of belief. Pantheism, when it finds a voice in words, usually takes one of two forms. There is the cool, unhurried logic of Spinoza, which appealed so strongly to Coleridge – Spinoza, who can speak of 'that eternal and infinite being we call God or nature' as if only a very unreasonable person would think of these as anything but synonyms. And there is the passionate eagerness of a writer like Richard Jefferies, who does not argue but expresses a feeling for sun and sea and the earth which can only be called religious. Wordsworth is obviously closer to Jefferies; indeed, without Wordsworth's poetry a book like *The Story of My Heart* could never have been written. Here is a typical passage of Jefferies. He has been climbing a hill and has reached the summit:

> I was utterly alone with the sun and the earth. Lying down on the grass, I spoke in my soul to the earth, the sun, the air, and the distant sea far beyond sight. I thought of the earth's firmness – I felt it bear me up; through the grassy couch there came an influence as if I could feel the great earth speaking to me. I thought of the wandering air – its pureness, which is its beauty; the air touched me and gave me something of itself. I spoke to the sea: though so far, in my mind I saw it, green at the rim of the earth and blue in deeper ocean; I desired to have its strength, its mystery and glory. Then I addressed the sun, desiring the soul equivalent of his light and brilliance, his endurance and unwearied race. I turned to the blue heaven over, gazing into its depth, inhaling its exquisite colour and sweetness. The rich blue of the unattainable flower of the sky drew my soul towards it, and there it rested, for pure colour is rest of heart. By all these I prayed; I felt an emotion of the soul beyond all definition; prayer is a puny thing to it, and the word is a rude sign to the feeling, but I know no other.[10]

To break off is not quite fair to Jefferies; his prose needs more space to breathe and move. But the quiet joy and the sense of the inadequacy of language are characteristic.

Jefferies' pleasure in the earth's firmness could be paralleled by an equally characteristic phrase in *The Prelude*, where Wordsworth, lying on the grass beneath a tree, finds himself

> soothed by a sense of touch
> From the warm ground, that balanced me, else lost
> Entirely.   (I.89)

The difference we feel between the two writers in a passage of any length is not just that Wordsworth's phrasing is more precise or that his rhythms have an energy disciplined by metre. It is a difference of conviction, or rather of consciousness.

Hints and suggestions of a life or spirit permeating the natural world are scattered, as we saw earlier, through the first two books of *The Prelude*. Yet when Wordsworth comes to speak directly of the One Life his tone, though not less passionate than Jefferies', is more complex. The key passages, chiefly two, were taken over from 'The Pedlar', and are best examined first in their original context.

V

'The Pedlar' grew out of 'The Ruined Cottage'. The original poem, the story of Margaret, was read to Coleridge at Racedown in June 1797. Between January and March 1798 Wordsworth enlarged it with a long account of the boyhood and youth of the Pedlar (who narrates Margaret's story).[11] On two occasions, probably December 1799 and December 1801, he then quarried this 'Pedlar' material for passages which he included, assigning them now to his own child-hood, in *The Prelude*. The relevant lines are these:

'The Pedlar'		*The Prelude*
Fragment (31 lines)	>	II.321–41
lines 203–222	>	II.416–34
lines 324–56	>	III.82, 122–9, 141–7, 156–67[12]

These 'Pedlar' lines, though we meet them fairly late in Book II and near the opening of Book III of *The Prelude*, were drafted at least eight months before the boyhood episodes in Book I – indeed, a few months before 'Tintern Abbey'. In many ways they are closer to 'Tintern Abbey', with its feeling for the One Life within us and abroad, than to anything in Book I of *The Prelude*. For Wordsworth in the spring of 1798 seems to have believed in the One Life, not indeed without moments of doubt, but with a passionate conviction he never quite felt again. The intellectual formulation, so far as he offers one, he probably owed to Coleridge, but the intuitions it supported and explained had their origin in his boyhood – a boyhood, as we know from *The Prelude*, much more profoundly shaped by nature than 'the coarser pleasures of my boyish days' so casually set aside in 'Tintern Abbey' would suggest.[13]

In two sequences of 'The Pedlar' the One Life is joyfully affirmed, in two others cautiously. The earliest of the four passages sounds an uncertain note:

> In the after day
> Of boyhood, many an hour in caves forlorn
> And in the hollow depths of naked crags
> He sate, and even in their fixed lineaments,
> Or from the power of a peculiar eye,
> Or by creative feeling overborne,
> Or by predominance of thought oppressed,
> Even in their fixed and steady lineaments
> He traced an ebbing and a flowing mind,
> Expression ever varying.   ('The Pedlar' 48–57)

There are no signs here of life as we ordinarily recognise it – no trees, plants or flowers, only crags and caves. And Wordsworth, keeping some distance from the experience, is evidently far from sure that the mind the young Pedlar traced in 'their fixed and steady lineaments' was really there. Perhaps it was only his intensely personal vision, or the stress of thought or feeling, that made him think so. Yet forty lines later we are reading this:

> Ere his ninth year he had been sent abroad
> To tend his father's sheep: such was his task
> Henceforward till the later day of youth.
> Oh then what soul was his, when on the tops
> Of the high mountains he beheld the sun
> Rise up and bathe the world in light. He looked,
> The ocean and the earth beneath him lay
> In gladness and deep joy. The clouds were touched,
> And in their silent faces did he read
> Unutterable love. Sound needed none,
> Nor any voice of joy: his spirit drank
> The spectacle. Sensation, soul and form
> All melted into him. They swallowed up
> His animal being. In them did he live,
> And by them did he live. They were his life.
> In such access of mind, in such high hour
> Of visitation from the living God,

He did not feel the God, he felt his works.
Thought was not: in enjoyment it expired.
                              `   ('The Pedlar' 92–110)

Emotion has almost overwhelmed the verse, so that logical
contradictions swim in the same element. Whatever 'sensation, soul and form' may mean, it is hard to see how they
could have 'melted into him' and at the same time swallowed
up his being. Yet the wonder and deep joy of the experience
are beyond question. Whatever Wordsworth thought or
didn't think ('Thought was not') at the time, we know what
he felt.

Neither of these two passages found a place in *The
Prelude*.[14] Within a hundred lines, however, we have a
paragraph that did:

> From Nature and her overflowing soul
> He had received so much that all his thoughts
> Were steeped in feeling. He was only then
> Contented when with bliss ineffable
> He felt the sentiment of being spread
> O'er all that moves, and all that seemeth still,
> O'er all which, lost beyond the reach of thought
> And human knowledge, to the human eye
> Invisible, yet liveth to the heart;
> O'er all that leaps, and runs, and shouts, and sings,
> Or beats the gladsome air; o'er all that glides
> Beneath the wave, yea, in the wave itself,
> And mighty depth of waters. Wonder not
> If such his transports were; for in all things
> He saw one life, and felt that it was joy.
>   ('The Pedlar' 204–18)

In *The Prelude*, with a change of pronoun from 'he' to 'I',
this appears as Book II, lines 416–30. What Wordsworth is
celebrating is not just the vitality of the organic world, though
the biblical echoes towards the close put the stress on that
vitality. The feeling of life as joy extends from all that moves
to 'all that seemeth still' (rocks, mountains), and what Wordsworth is speaking of is something 'ineffable', something
'beyond the reach of thought', which convinces not by a flash
of insight but by the fact that it 'liveth to the heart'.

Two points are worth making here. First, for all the vigour of the rhythm, which wakens our sympathy with the plenitude of life, no specific creatures are mentioned – and no one familiar with Wordsworth's poetry would expect them to be. Nature to Wordsworth means lakes and mountains, wind, cloud and sky. (He has a few poems about birds, but the finest of these, 'To the Cuckoo', is a purely visionary poem). The other point of interest is the line: 'O'er all that leaps, and runs, and shouts, and sings.' The one creature that leaps and runs and shouts and sings is surely a small boy. Is Wordsworth remembering a time when he unconsciously projected his own vitality into everything he saw? Very likely, though at this point in 'The Pedlar' he gives no sign of recognising that possibility. The tone, it is true, is not quite that of the sunrise paragraph: the 'Unutterable love', the sense of a visitation from the living God, have gone. Essentially, however, the sunrise lines and the exultant 'sentiment of being' passage are in accord. Neither subjects the experience of the One Life to scrutiny. An overflow of complete happiness, and the delight of finding words to recapture it, are enough.

Yet three pages later the note of hesitation which Wordsworth had sounded near the beginning of 'The Pedlar' returns:

> From deep analogies by thought supplied,
> Or consciousnesses not to be subdued,
> To every natural form, rock, fruit, and flower,
> Even the loose stones that cover the highway,
> He gave a moral life; he saw them feel,
> Or linked them to some feeling. In all shapes
> He found a secret and mysterious soul,
> A fragrance and a Spirit of strange meaning.
> Though poor in outward shew, he was most rich:
> He had a world about him – 'twas his own,
> He made it – for it only lived to him,
> And to the God who looked into his mind.
>
> ('The Pedlar' 330–41)

Wordsworth is struggling to understand his experience, and the writing could hardly be more tentative. To every rock, fruit and flower, 'He gave a moral life; he saw them feel . . .'

Gave or saw? (It can hardly be both.) In all shapes he 'found'
a secret and mysterious soul; yet this world, so full of life and
meaning, was his precisely because 'He made it – for it only
lived to him / And to the God who looked into his mind.'

What are we to make of this? Evidently even in the spring
of 1798, when he could still recall the unreflective joy he had
known at times in boyhood, Wordsworth could only intermittently believe that this joy gave him access to a spirit that
animates 'all objects of all thought'. By the summer of that
year the mood of 'Tintern Abbey' ('If this / Be but a vain
belief') is almost elegiac: 'Whose dwelling is the light of
setting suns' looks forward to the close of the 'Immortality
Ode' rather than back to the young Pedlar's rapture as he
saw the sun rise and 'bathe the world in light'.

Since the river of Wordsworth's mind so often turned back
on itself, a few landmarks may be helpful at this point:

'The Pedlar'		January/March 1798
'Tintern Abbey'		July 1798
The Prelude	Book I (childhood episodes)	Oct. 1798/Feb. 1799
	Book II (mostly)	Sept./Dec. 1799
	Book III.1–167	probably Dec. 1801

I mentioned that about the end of the year 1799, and again
(probably) in December 1801, Wordsworth incorporated
some of his 'Pedlar' verse into *The Prelude*. What happens is
interesting.

Towards the end of Book II of *The Prelude* Wordsworth has
been speaking of his pleasure in searching out affinities in
nature between objects apparently unrelated. He goes on:

> My seventeenth year was come,
> And, whether from this habit rooted now
> So deeply in my mind, or from excess
> Of the great social principle of life
> Coercing all things into sympathy,
> To unorganic natures I transferred
> My own enjoyments, or, the power of truth
> Coming in revelation, I conversed

> With things that really are, I at this time
> Saw blessings spread around me like a sea.   (II. 405)

Here are at least two, perhaps three, alternatives. Either the
One Life was a reality – 'the power of truth / Coming in
revelation' – or it was a projection of Wordsworth's mind,
whether from his eagerness to find affinities in nature or from
sheer excess of sympathetic feeling. Which of these expla-
nations is the most likely? Wordsworth is clearly unwilling to
decide. His 'whether . . . or . . . or . . .', like Coleridge's
'And what if . . .?' in 'The Eolian Harp', is the strategy of a
writer for whom it matters more to keep open the possibility
of deeper insight than to commit himself to a decision that
satisfies (if it does) the intellect alone. Keats, so often critical
of Wordsworth, would have approved.

What makes the passage more puzzling when we are
reading *The Prelude* is that Wordsworth, leaving his dilemma
unresolved, moves straight into:

> Thus did my days pass on, and now at length
> From Nature and her overflowing soul
> I had received so much that all my thoughts
> Were steeped in feeling   (II.415)

and reproduces, almost word for word, the 'sentiment of
being' lines from 'The Pedlar'.

These lines, which I quoted earlier (p.24) are the only full
celebration of the One Life in *The Prelude*. And the doubt with
which they are introduced ('whether . . . or . . . or . . .')
returns at the close. Almost immediately after 'Wonder not /
If such my transports were, for in all things / I saw one life,
and felt that it was joy' (II.428), Wordsworth adds: 'If this be
error, and another faith / Find easier access to the pious mind
. . .' (II.435).[15] If this be error? 'The Pedlar', at that point, had
no such misgivings.

Undercut by the lines that introduce it, and shadowed by
the phrase that follows ('If this be error'), the One Life is put
in question again a few pages later in *The Prelude*. Here, just
after the beginning of Book III, Wordsworth draws on the
fourth passage I quoted from 'The Pedlar':

> From deep analogies by thought supplied,
> Or consciousnesses not to be subdued,
> To every natural form, rock, fruit or flower,
> Even the loose stones that cover the highway,
> I gave a moral life – I saw them feel,
> Or linked them to some feeling.   (III.122)

We are back to the bewildered 'or . . . or . . .'. And the uncertainty is not dispelled by the next sentence:

>   The great mass
> Lay bedded in a quickening soul, and all
> That I beheld respired with inward meaning.   (III.127)

In itself this sounds unequivocal. But what it claims is an independent reality for the life Wordsworth has just been saying may be a projection of his own mind.

One sees why Coleridge's hopes that *The Recluse* would be the first true philosophical poem were bound to be disappointed. Except at moments, when he managed to recover and find words for a joy he had known occasionally in boyhood, Wordsworth could never be sure of the One Life. It might be a reality. It might, as Coleridge acknowledges sadly in 'Dejection', be an illusion.

References to the One Life can be found here and there in later books of *The Prelude*. In Book V we read of poems as powers to be 'hallowed' only less than 'Nature's self which is the breath of God' (V.222). 'Or', as the 1850 text cautiously adds, 'his pure Word by miracle revealed'. Travelling through France to reach the Alps in his last vacation from Cambridge, Wordsworth still felt 'the ever-living universe' (VI.701) as a presence. In Book VIII, looking back again, he remembers boyhood and youth as a time when

> The pulse of being everywhere was felt,
> When all the several frames of things, like stars
> Through every magnitude distinguishable,
> Were half confounded in each other's blaze,
> One galaxy of life and joy.   (VIII.627)

Later, reproaching himself with that sensuous delight he had
taken in landscape in the summer of 1793, he cries:

> O soul of Nature, that dost overflow
> With passion and with life, what feeble men
> Walk on this earth, how feeble have I been
> When thou wert in thy strength![16]   (XI.146)

And in the last book, with Coleridge affectionately in mind,
he speaks of

> the life
> Of all things and the mighty unity
> In all which we behold, and feel, and are.   (XIII.253)

These later references to the One Life all date from 1804/5,
when the bulk of *The Prelude* was written. Isolated and
abstract, they have neither the rhythmic energy nor the
immediacy of the first two books, and in a poem of well over
8,000 lines they do not, of course, count for much. At most
they suggest that the idea still meant something to Wordsworth. Neither then nor later was he ready to deny the One
Life: to affirm, as Coleridge does in 'Dejection', that 'in our
life alone does Nature live'. But only in the spring and
summer of 1798, in 'The Pedlar' and one or two of the *Lyrical
Ballads*, especially 'Tintern Abbey', does he speak of the One
Life with real conviction; and even in 'The Pedlar' joy is
hedged with doubts. In the winter of 1798/99, when the
childhood episodes of *The Prelude* were written, there are still,
as we saw, hints and suggestions of a life everywhere in
nature. By 1804/5 conviction has dwindled into belief, and
then fades or survives only as assertion.[17]

Had Wordsworth wished to offer a philosophic system –
the kind of thing Coleridge had in mind when *The Recluse*
was first mooted in 1797/98 – he might no doubt have gone
through *The Prelude* to bring different passages more closely
into line with each other. Fortunately his attempts to tone
down the pantheism of 1798 with the Christian piety of later
years were sporadic, and consist for the most part of additions
rather than cuts. The result, even in 1850, is a more absorbing,
though a more confusing poem, than the one Coleridge
would have preferred him to write.

2

The Mind and the World

The mind, that ocean

Marvell

Après tout, le monde est autour de moi,
non devant moi.

Merleau-Ponty

The joyous sense of the One Life Wordsworth knew occasionally in boyhood, and again in the spring and summer of 1798, was of a life in which he shared. His doubts about that life – was it simply a projection of his own vitality? – were therefore linked with, and perhaps intensified by, a further question: what is the right relationship between the mind and the world in which it lives? How, for that matter, does the mind make contact with a world of objects at all?

The boyhood incidents he recalls in the first book of *The Prelude* – climbing for ravens' eggs, skating under the stars, and so on – are all of a time when the mind was still unconscious of itself (he was not yet ten years old). *The Prelude* traces the growth of consciousness. Not just the growth of a poet's mind, for the poet, as Wordsworth says in the Preface to *Lyrical Ballads*, is a man speaking to men. If he differs from his readers, being endowed with 'a more lively sensibility' and greater powers of expression, it is only in degree, not in kind. Wordsworth therefore has no hesitation in generalising, in taking his own experience, unique though he knew it to be, as representative. And since *The Prelude* is addressed to a fellow-poet (Coleridge) he can do this in a tone that looks for understanding and agreement.

When Wordsworth speaks of the mind, especially in the early books of *The Prelude*, he is usually thinking not of the intellect, but of the life of feeling. In Book I, after the raven's nest paragraph, he writes:

> The mind of man is framed even like the breath
> And harmony of music. There is a dark
> Invisible workmanship that reconciles
> Discordant elements, and makes them move
> In one society.   (I.351)

No doubt Wordsworth would have agreed that this society includes the ability to analyse, compare, make deductions and moral judgements. But these are not, for him, what matters. The essential elements reconciled in the growing mind are the joys, excited hopes and terrors of childhood: for it is these that have formed what Wordsworth values in the man and poet he has become.

Childhood is important for any writer. It is the time when he sees the world most clearly, when his first attachments are formed, when he becomes conscious of his own identity and his own solitude. But for no other poet, not even Rilke, has childhood had the importance it came to have for Wordsworth. There were good reasons for this, and not only the fact, which he discovered when writing 'The Pedlar' and *The Prelude*, that the springs of his imaginative power were to be found there. The passion of his childhood was nature, and it was love of nature, Wordsworth believed, that led him to love man. It was love of nature also, both in itself and in the renewed conviction it gave him of the value of feeling, that was decisive in his recovery from the crisis years 1793–96.

Books X–XII of *The Prelude* are devoted to that crisis. We shall be looking at it in the next chapter. For the moment it is enough to recall that one element in it was Wordsworth's attachment for a year or two to the rationalism of Godwin, and his revulsion from that rationalism as the Terror in France and then French aggression in Holland, Italy and Spain, destroyed his faith in the Revolution. Racedown (1795–97) and Alfoxden (1797–98) saw Wordsworth's recovery. What he now learned to value again, as he tells us in Book XII, was not reason but 'the great and simple affections of our nature' which he defends and reaffirms in the Preface to *Lyrical Ballads*.

This deep conviction of the value of feeling, this trust in the human heart, is central to Wordsworth's poetry. The

child is father of the man: what we are, we are by virtue of
those first affections which are 'the fountain light of all our
day'. And therefore nothing in later life has the significance
of those early years when the man was still a child.

I

In childhood mind and body are more intimately related than
they are ever likely to be again, and the presence of an
outside world is at first taken for granted. Hills are there to
be climbed, streams are there to fish in, woods to search for
hazel nuts. Wordsworth's re-creation of that world has a
marvellous freshness and precision, a fidelity not just to
sensory experience but above all to the emotions of the child.
His claim that poetry is the spontaneous overflow of powerful feelings is not often quoted in full. The claim occurs twice
in the Preface to *Lyrical Ballads*. At its first appearance
Wordsworth adds an important rider: that a good poet is also
a man who has thought long and deeply. Some pages later,
when he brings the phrase forward again, he explains how
(in his experience) poems get written: 'I have said that poetry
is the spontaneous overflow of powerful feelings: it takes its
origin from emotion recollected in tranquillity.' So much for
the origin of a poem. Then what happens?

> The emotion is contemplated till by a species of reaction
> the tranquillity disappears, and an emotion, kindred to
> that which was before the subject of contemplation, is
> gradually produced and does itself actually exist in the
> mind.

In this mood – not a mood of tranquillity, but one of powerful
feeling – successful composition generally begins and is
carried through.

Any of the great sequences in the first two books of *The
Prelude* would illustrate this. What makes the skating lines,
for example, so exhilarating is not just the cutting edge of word
and phrase, though the writing is astonishingly onomatopoeic.
It is the way the whole movement of the paragraph has been
generated and sustained by an emotion urgently felt:

> And in the frosty season, when the sun
> Was set, and visible for many a mile

The cottage windows through the twilight blazed,
I heeded not the summons; happy time
It was indeed for all of us, to me
It was a time of rapture. Clear and loud
The village clock tolled six; I wheeled about
Proud and exulting, like an untired horse
That cares not for its home. All shod with steel
We hissed along the polished ice in games
Confederate, imitative of the chace
And woodland pleasures, the resounding horn,
The pack loud bellowing, and the hunted hare.
So through the darkness and the cold we flew,
And not a voice was idle. With the din,
Meanwhile, the precipices rang aloud;
The leafless trees and every icy crag
Tinkled like iron; while the distant hills
Into the tumult sent an alien sound
Of melancholy, not unnoticed; while the stars,
Eastward, were sparkling clear, and in the west
The orange sky of evening died away.   (I.452)

The quality of perception there is as sharp as anything in
Hopkins – was it the untired horse that prompted the brilliant
'shod with steel' in the next line? But the evocativeness of the
writing owes at least as much to the finely judged line-breaks,
the apparently effortless strength of syntax and the energy of
the rhythm. Evidently the emotion of twenty years earlier, or
something very like it, has revived and actually exists in
Wordsworth's mind. A moment later, in a quiet enlargement
of experience – the kind of enlargement that happens more
than once in *The Prelude* – the scene closes with the characteristically Wordsworthian feeling for the earth turning in space:

And oftentimes
When we had given our bodies to the wind,
And all the shadowy banks on either side
Came sweeping through the darkness, spinning still
The rapid line of motion, then at once
Have I, reclining back upon my heels,
Stopped short – yet still the solitary cliffs

> Wheeled by me, even as if the earth had rolled
> With visible motion her diurnal round.   (I.478)

The feeling that holds together the several episodes in the
first book of *The Prelude* is not nostalgia but gratitude: to the
Derwent, 'fairest of all rivers', and then to the woods, lakes
and mountains of 'that beloved vale' to which Wordsworth
was 'transplanted'. Often he was out after dark, when the
hills seem larger. One night, when he had taken a small boat
out on Ullswater, a crag till then hidden by the skyline
suddenly confronted him:

>   I struck and struck again,
> And, growing still in stature, the huge cliff
> Rose up between me and the stars, and still
> With measured motion, like a living thing
> Strode after me.   (I.408)

The anxiety of guilt (he had borrowed the boat without
permission) was heightened by a small boy's sense, still
vague, of the universe as vast and mysterious, so that for
many days no familiar images of trees, sky or fields were in
his thoughts:

> But huge and mighty forms that do not live
> Like living men moved slowly through my mind
> By day, and were the trouble of my dreams.   (I.425)

When we recall this sequence we think of the mystery and
power of that ending. But the ending is all the more disturbing
for the accuracy of the writing a little earlier, where Wordsworth remembers the dripping of the lifted oars between
each stroke and the next:

>   It was an act of stealth
> And troubled pleasure. Nor without the voice
> Of mountain-echoes did my boat move on,
> Leaving behind her still on either side
> Small circles glittering idly in the moon,
> Until they melted all into one track
> Of sparkling light.   (I.388)

As in the skating lines, the whole body is engaged, not just
the eye:

> lustily
> I dipped my oars into the silent lake,
> And as I rose upon the stroke my boat
> Went heaving through the water like a swan.   (I.401)

Sight and sound are strengthened by memories of touch, gesture and movement, and no gap in time or consciousness, until the close of the paragraph, separates the body's life ('And as I rose upon the stroke') from the emotions of the mind.

Wordsworth's strongest emotions, like any child's, were chiefly two: joy and fear. These could be simultaneous, heightening each other:

> Oh, when I have hung
> Above the raven's nest, by knots of grass
> And half-inch fissures in the slippery rock
> But ill sustained, and almost, as it seemed,
> Suspended by the blast which blew amain,
> Shouldering the naked crag, oh, at that time
> While on the perilous ridge I hung alone,
> With what strange utterance did the loud dry wind
> Blow through my ears; the sky seemed not a sky
> Of earth, and with what motion moved the clouds!   (I.341)

The force of the writing springs from a sense of world and body as at once resisting and supporting each other. Yet beyond the precision of which language is capable there hovers a sense of the world itself, and the body with it, at risk in space: a dawning perception, therefore, of nature and the human mind as separate, thinly divided from each other by the body.

II

In Book II this awareness deepens, as nature, till now incidental to the small boy's climbing, swimming and riding, is sought for her own sake. There is no straightforward development, no attempt to arrange the incidents in chronological sequence, and this makes the writing convincingly true to life – both to the irregularity of events (roughly from Wordsworth's tenth to his seventeenth year) and to the way that memory recalls them. But Wordsworth wants to under-

stand, not just remember, the past. Half way through Book
II, therefore, he widens his enquiry by tracing human perception back to the first stirrings of consciousness. Nursed in its
mother's arms, the infant babe responds to her affection:

> Such feelings pass into his torpid life
> Like an awakening breeze, and hence his mind,
> Even in the first trial of its powers,
> Is prompt and watchful, eager to combine
> In one appearance all the elements
> And parts of the same object, else detached
> And loth to coalesce.   (II.244)

'Torpid' captures beautifully the intensely physical life of the
babe, which is still so largely a life of sucking, sleeping and
slowly becoming aware of its own body. What quickens this
torpid sensibility is the mother's love. Animated by that, the
infant mind grasps the unity of objects in the outside world
for the first time: the mother's arms, breast and eyes, 'coalesce'
in one beloved presence; the flower becomes a flower, with
stalk and petals, not just a blur of green and yellow. And
with this the child, 'creator and receiver both', finds himself
gradually at home on the earth, not a stranger to it:

> No outcast he, bewildered and depressed;
> Along his infant veins are interfused
> The gravitation and the filial bond
> Of Nature that connect him with the world.   (II.261)

The whole paragraph (it runs to more than forty lines) brings
into sudden focus Wordsworth's conviction that the relationship between Nature and the mind is one of mutual depend-
ence. Ontologically they are equally real; neither has, nor
should have, priority. And in this relationship the mind,
even in the first weeks of life,

> Creates, creator and receiver both,
> Working but in alliance with the works
> Which it beholds.   (II.273)

The question to which Wordsworth has been sketching an
answer, or the beginnings of an answer, had been central to
the problem of our knowledge of the world since Descartes.

For the eye is only a lens, though a very complex one. It records sensations, not perceptions. How are these sensations translated into images of the rocks, hills, trees and so on, which (presumably) exist outside us?

Locke, the authority on such matters for the eighteenth century, is not always clear on this point. Often he uses the terms 'sensation' and 'perception' as if they were interchangeable, at other times he seems to think of the understanding as in some way converting sensations into perceptions. The distinction he draws between primary and secondary qualities implies that the mind contributes something to our experience, but Locke would not have said, as Young does in the line Wordsworth vaguely remembered when he was composing 'Tintern Abbey', that our senses 'half create the wondrous world they see'. In principle, for Locke, the mind is passive in perception: a mirror, not a lamp. ('It is but opening the eye', Addison observes, 'and the scene enters'.)[1] Hartley, through whom Locke's arguments reached Wordsworth, agreed. The senses provide the groundwork of all our knowledge, and by association, according to Hartley, habits of thought and feeling are formed which build up the ever-growing structure of the mind.

Wordsworth's debt to Hartley is apparent in the first book of *The Prelude*, and even clearer in the Preface to *Lyrical Ballads*. For Wordsworth, however, the dichotomy of active/passive is too simple. His liking for the word 'creative', in preference to 'active', can be confusing, but 'recipient' (II.252) rather than 'passive' defines his meaning admirably. More than most poets Wordsworth is a contemplative – 'gaze' is one of his favourite verbs – and in contemplation the mind is at once receptive and energetic. In his first year at Cambridge, he tells us,

> whatsoe'er of terror, or of love,
> Or beauty, Nature's daily face put on
> From transitory passion, unto this
> I was as wakeful even as waters are
> To the sky's motion, in a kindred sense
> Of passion was obedient as a lute
> That waits upon the touches of the wind.   (III.132)

The lute sounds like a recollection of Coleridge's poem, 'The Eolian Harp', and without the image of sky and water (unmistakably Wordsworth's own) which so beautifully modifies it, might be taken to imply Hartley's conception of the mind. The mood of Wordsworth's lines, however, is not at all that of Coleridge's speculations. Characteristically, Coleridge moves from the psychological (his own musings) to the metaphysical:

> And what if all of animated nature
> Be but organic harps diversely framed,
> That tremble into thought, as o'er them sweeps
> Plastic and vast, one intellectual breeze,
> At once the soul of each, and God of all?

Wordsworth stays with his own experience, and any hint that the mind is merely passive in perception is challenged by the overtones of word and phrase. Water, it is true, can only reflect the sky, but 'wakeful' suggests that these waters are more than ready to do this, and the sky (as so often with Wordsworth) is in motion. The effect of Wordsworth's lines is not to suggest that the mind is passive, but rather to confirm that his youthful sensibility was keenly attentive and alive. Coleridge's poem speaks of idle fantasies that 'Traverse my indolent and passive brain'. Wordsworth, even at his most Hartleian, would never have said that. For him the mind is not just an instrument, but an instrument alert to every touch of the wind as waters are responsive to every movement of the clouds.[2]

III

I said that for Wordsworth the relationship between nature and the mind is one of equals, that neither has nor should have priority. It is one thing, however, to say this, another to prove it.

The poetry of relationship finds its most memorable expression in the Boy of Winander lines, now in Book V though drafted at the same time as the childhood episodes of Book I. The passage is worth quoting in full:

> There was a boy – ye knew him well, ye cliffs
> And islands of Winander – many a time

At evening, when the stars had just begun
To move along the edges of the hills,
Rising or setting, would he stand alone
Beneath the trees or by the glimmering lake,
And there, with fingers interwoven, both hands
Pressed closely palm to palm, and to his mouth
Uplifted, he as through an instrument
Blew mimic hootings to the silent owls
That they might answer him. And they would shout
Across the wat'ry vale, and shout again,
Responsive to his call, with quivering peals
And long halloos, and screams, and echoes loud,
Redoubled and redoubled – concourse wild
Of mirth and jocund din. And when it chanced
That pauses of deep silence mocked his skill,
Then sometimes in that silence, while he hung
Listening, a gentle shock of mild surprize
Has carried far into his heart the voice
Of mountain torrents; or the visible scene
Would enter unwares into his mind
With all its solemn imagery, its rocks,
Its woods, and that uncertain heaven, received
Into the bosom of the steady lake.   (V.389)

The half-human cry of the owls, the pauses of deep silence, the expectancy of 'while he hung / Listening' prepare us for the slight shock of surprise that carries 'far into his heart' the voice of mountain torrents. Mind and lake are almost, not quite, identified with each other at the close. Yet the mind is more than a mirror. Like the lake, it does not just reflect the imagery of rocks, trees and cloud, but receives them into its depths. This may sound dangerously close to 'the abyss of idealism'. Perhaps it is.[3] But the poetry stops at the edge of the abyss. Sky, rock and woods are still there, outside the boy's mind. The owls, though they have fallen silent, are still there.

The creative mind and the world exist in relationship; but a relationship can always break down. The mind may seek to appropriate the world, or surrender to it.

In *The Prelude*, even where the writing is most fully pantheistic, there is no complete surrender to the natural world.

The poet who affirms and rejoices in the One Life (II.405–34) nevertheless stands a little outside it, remembering and questioning. The opposite danger, that the mind may absorb the world, is the one unconsciously risked by the Boy of Winander. Wordsworth knew it intimately. Many years later he could still recall days in boyhood when what he saw seemed only a landscape in the mind:

> I was often unable to think of external things as having external existence, and I communed with all that I saw as something not apart from, but inherent in, my own immaterial nature. Many times while going to school have I grasped at a wall or tree to recall myself from this abyss of idealism to the reality.[4]

In *The Prelude* there is a wonderful moment in Book II when Wordsworth remembers one of the long summer evenings on Windermere:

> But ere the fall
> Of night, when in our pinnace we returned
> Over the dusky lake, and to the beach
> Of some small island steered our course, with one,
> The minstrel of our troop, and left him there,
> And rowed off gently, while he blew his flute
> Alone upon the rock, oh, then the calm
> And dead still water lay upon my mind
> Even with a weight of pleasure, and the sky,
> Never before so beautiful, sank down
> Into my heart and held me like a dream.   (II.170)

More often he was alone. Later in the same book he speaks of boyhood walks round Esthwaite just after daybreak, 'when the vale / Lay quiet in an utter solitude' (II.363). There, sitting on a rock among the hills,

> such a holy calm
> Did overspread my soul that I forgot
> That I had bodily eyes, and what I saw
> Appeared like something in myself, a dream,
> A prospect in my mind.   (II.367)

At every reading of *The Prelude* we are struck by the frequency with which that phrase 'my mind' falls into place either (as here) to close a cadence or at the end of a line, as if Wordsworth has paused to brood over the words. Often he prefers to write 'the mind': not, I think, or not always, because he is eager to claim that his experience was typical, but because he obscurely feels his mind as something separate from himself – and something to be feared. The poet, he tells Coleridge in the preamble to Book I, has times when 'the mind itself, / The meditative mind' (I.149) disturbs him. And in Book VI, thinking of Coleridge's absorption as an undergraduate in Platonism and scholastic philosophy, in words rather than things, he sees such studies as 'The self-created sustenance of a mind / Debarred from Nature's living images' (VI.312).

'The Pedlar', which often anticipates *The Prelude*, suggests that there were times in boyhood when Wordsworth too lost touch with 'Nature's living images'. This comes through even in one or two of the poems written at Hawkshead. Marvell was not much read in the eighteenth century, but Wordsworth was surely remembering his splendid metaphor of the mind as an ocean when he wrote (while still at school) a little elegy for a dog. The dog was a 'rough terrier of the hills' that accompanied him on his walks, and Wordsworth recalls how the birth of some lovely, unexpected image would bring them together:

> If, while I gaz'd to Nature blind,
> In the calm ocean of my mind
> Some new-created image rose
> In full-grown beauty at its birth
> Lovely as Venus from the sea,
> Then, while my glad hand sprung to thee,
> We were the happiest pair on earth.[5]

Wordsworth was not often 'to Nature blind'. When he was, it was usually, as here, because his mind was at its most active.

The elegy is hardly more than a fragment, but Wordsworth valued those last few lines enough to rewrite them for *The Prelude*:

> A hundred times when in these wanderings
> I have been busy with the toil of verse –

Great pains and little progress – and at once
Some fair enchanting image in my mind
Rose up, full-formed like Venus from the sea,
Have I sprung forth towards him and let loose
My hand upon his back with stormy joy,
Caressing him again and yet again.   (IV.101)

Probably the act of touch was important: not just a release of affection and delight, though of course it was chiefly that, but a reassurance – as with the wall or tree that saved him from the abyss of idealism.

The Prelude is a sustained meditation of the mind on its own nature, its origin and powers. Occasionally Wordsworth sees his mind as a river, fed by tributaries not always traceable to their source. Always he recognises that there is something elusive, something beyond our comprehension, about the mind. At Cambridge, though the months of casual study passed agreeably enough, 'Caverns there were within my mind / Which sun could never penetrate' (III.246). And the two most elaborate similes in the poem, the cave in Book VIII (711–27) and the boat gliding over the surface of past time in Book IV (247–64), are essays in scepticism and patience as the mind tries quietly to distinguish shadow from substance, appearance from reality.

If Wordsworth ever doubted the potency of the mind, he had it regularly brought home to him by the vividness of his dreams – not only in boyhood, as after the night with the stolen boat, but later. For Locke and the eighteenth century the mind meant the conscious mind, the power of reason. Wordsworth knew something of the disturbing energies of the unconscious. For years after the September massacres and the atrocities of the Terror in France he woke from nightmares in which he struggled to plead 'before unjust tribunals' (X.377). On Salisbury Plain, in broad daylight, he had visions of Druid priests and human sacrifice (XII.312–53). And the dream in Book V of *The Prelude*, one of the great passages in the poem, has a strange, compelling clarity and power. The rider, half Bedouin, half Don Quixote, has been crazed by 'internal thought / Protracted among endless solitudes' (V.145), yet what Wordsworth feels for him is not so much pity as a kind of reverence, a feeling that 'in the blind and awful lair / Of such a madness reason did lie couched' (V.151). The genesis of the dream, according to Wordsworth, lay in his dismay that something so material, and therefore so easily destroyed, as books should have to be trusted with the supreme achievements of the human spirit. Before he fell asleep he had been meditating on poetry and 'geometric truth'. One of the books that the Arab carries with him (the stone) is Euclid's *Elements*, and though plainly of less worth than the shell it is still precious. From his room in Cambridge, on moonlit nights, Wordsworth could see the antechapel of Trinity and the statue 'Of Newton with his prism and silent face' (III.59) – the index of a mind as solitary as his own.

Wordsworth's feelings about science were ambivalent. The appeal that mathematics, especially geometry, held for him seems to have been twofold. As a world of pure intelligence it offered ample evidence of the reach of the mind. At the same time, to a consciousness like his own – 'a mind beset / With images, and haunted by itself' (VI.179) – it came as a relief to find a structure of ideas so purely theoretic and internally coherent. It was to mathematics, therefore, that he turned again in the months of his despairing reaction from the rationalism of Godwin. But in these months Wordsworth knew also the precariousness of the mind. In *The Borderers* (1796/97) the intellectual power goes 'sounding on / Through words and things, a dim and perilous way' (Act IV, lines 1774–5). And it was just before or after *The Borderers* that Wordsworth wrote the bleak and eerie fragment, 'Incipient Madness'.[6] The title, his own, is doubtless a sign of sanity. The fragment itself is a reminder of Johnson's, or at any rate Imlac's, warning: that of all the uncertainties of our life the most dreadful is the uncertain continuance of reason.[7]

IV

What made the relationship of the mind to the world so important, and so problematic, for Wordsworth was not just the narrowness of the ridge he sometimes walked between the abyss of idealism and the gulf of pantheism. There is also in his poetry a tension between Wordsworth's certainty of the worth of feeling and a stubbornly matter-of-fact strain in his temperament. Of this, the strongly empirical bias of his mind (or rather part of his mind), the evidence is everywhere in his work. One sign of it is the prosaic attention to detail which provoked the derision of his contemporaries. Another is the simple strength of a poem like 'Michael' or 'The Ruined Cottage'. Wordsworth has a deep respect for objects, especially for objects in nature that endure. One reason for his choice of rural life as the setting for most of the *Lyrical Ballads* was that 'in that condition the passions of men are incorporated with the beautiful and permanent forms of nature'. Of course these forms are 'permanent' only in comparison with our own brief lives, but Wordsworth's choice of that word is revealing. The power of one of his greatest poems lies in his sense of the tragic disparity between the transience of human life and the apparent permanence of the world:

> No motion has she now, no force;
> She neither hears nor sees,
> Rolled round in earth's diurnal course
> With rocks and stones and trees.

As soon as the mind becomes fully conscious, it finds itself in an ever-changing relationship with rocks and trees. Any relationship is a balance, often delicate and unstable. Between two people it depends on mutual respect, recognition of the other as a centre of equal value. With nature, the whole responsibility for the relationship rests with man, and various adjustments of the balance are possible – those made, for example, by the farmer, the botanist, or the civil engineer. To some men nature presents itself as an obstacle, to others simply as a context for human life. To the poet, nature is a world with its own life, infinitely larger than ours and encompassing ours.

So long as the poet is content to describe this world there is no problem, though there are difficulties. First, he has to learn to see the world – not so easy a matter as we sometimes suppose. 'Hundreds of people can talk for one who can think', said Ruskin, 'but thousands can think for one who can see'.[8] That is, see clearly, not with the lethargy of habit. Then the poet has to find words and rhythms for what he sees:

> meanwhile the calm lake
> Grew dark, with all the shadows on its breast,
> And now and then a fish up-leaping snapped
> The breathless stillness.   (V.463)

Accuracy of this kind is rare and valuable. But in a good poem accuracy is incidental to a larger purpose, the expression (and exploration) of feeling and thought. Without feeling the rhythm will be mechanical, the tinkle of a musical box. Indeed, unless he feels something for his subject, why should the poet write about it at all? Why choose one subject rather than another, the Wye valley rather than the Quantocks or the Malvern Hills?

Poetry, then, springs from feeling. Yet once his emotions are engaged, once the poet responds to nature – and Words-worth wanted a poetry of response – perception will often be disturbed. The vision may be more intense; it will certainly be more subjective. Painting faces the same dilemma. Frequently, though by no means always, landscape painting gives priority to the outside world of earth and sky. The result is realism, including Impressionism: Constable, Corot, Monet. At the other extreme the mind takes charge, flooding the natural scene with its own energies. The result is a more expressionist art: Van Gogh, say, or even Edvard Munch. Of course there is feeling in Constable and Corot, but essentially what their painting expresses is a calm, disinterested love of the visible world. Van Gogh's love is more vehement: dis-tress, passion and frustrated passion, jostle (so to speak) the lens through which he sees the world.

So with poetry. When the world is given priority, we get the direct, often lively detail of a poet like John Clare. When the mind asserts itself, poetry moves either in the direction of the pathetic fallacy (the ascription of human emotion to natural objects) or towards the use of landscape, weather and season as an objective correlative for human feeling.[9] Obviously any generalisation as large as this would need qualifying. Hopkins is at once passionate and brilliantly precise. Edward Thomas, Stevens and other poets since Hopkins, have tried to find a balance, at once moral and spiritual (not just aesthetic – the whole man is engaged) between truth to the life of feeling and fidelity to nature. The balance is a precarious one. If the emotions are indulged, we get a rush of excitement, not a poem. When emotion is too firmly restrained, we are back with accuracy for its own sake.

In *The Prelude* the balance is held most delicately, not without dips and tremors, in the early books. There is a beautiful example in Book IV, where Wordsworth, returning to Hawkshead after his first year at Cambridge, finds himself happily lying down again in the bed he had slept in as a boy:

> that bed where I so oft
> Had lain awake on breezy nights to watch
> The moon in splendour couched among the leaves
> Of a tall ash that near our cottage stood,
> Had watched her with fixed eyes, while to and fro
> In the dark summit of the moving tree
> She rocked with every impulse of the wind.   (IV.77)

This truth at once to the world and to the life of feeling was not achieved easily. Wordsworth's early verse often drives towards one or other of the two extremes, and the balance held in *The Prelude* will be more apparent if we look briefly at the longest of these early poems, *An Evening Walk* and *Descriptive Sketches of the Alps*.[10] Both were published in 1793, just after Wordsworth's return from France, though *An Evening Walk*, which is much the stronger poem, had been drafted a year or two before.

An Evening Walk, a poem of about 400 lines, reworks material from 'The Vale of Esthwaite', the most ambitious of Wordsworth's schoolboy efforts. In phrasing it owes a good deal, naturally, to earlier poets. Of the scenes depicted, on the other hand, every detail is one that Wordsworth had noticed himself. 'There is not an image in it', he told Miss Fenwick, 'which I have not observed'. To observe, however, is one thing; to describe, another. Even after its publication *An Evening Walk* was frequently revised. One passage gave Wordsworth particular trouble:

> Now while the solemn evening shadows sail
> On red slow-waving pinions down the vale,

> And, fronting the bright west in stronger lines,
> The oak its dark'ning boughs and foliage twines,
> I love beside the glowing lake to stray
> Where winds the road along the secret bay.
>
> (1793, 191–6)

This is less diffuse than it had been in 'The Vale of Esthwaite' but the first couplet, pointedly reminding us that shadows are not always grey, draws attention to itself. What Wordsworth really wanted to get clear, what had delighted him as a boy, was the boldness with which the structure of the oak is defined at evening by the brightness of the western sky. In revision, therefore, the red shadows are sacrificed, 'slow-waving' becomes the more natural 'slowly-waving', and the oak, promoted to the first line of its couplet, is further set against the sky by the demonstrative 'yon':

> Now while the solemn evening shadows sail
> On slowly-waving pinions down the vale,
> And, fronting the bright west, yon oak entwines
> Its darkening boughs and leaves in stronger lines,
> 'Tis pleasant near the tranquil lake to stray
> Where, winding on . . . (etc.)
>
> (1836, 211–16)

Wordsworth was still not satisfied. The image, he told Miss Fenwick, is feebly and imperfectly expressed. Nevertheless, it was one he valued:

> I recollect distinctly the very spot where this first struck me. It was in the way between Hawkshead and Ambleside, and gave me extreme pleasure. The moment was important in my poetical history; for I date from it my consciousness of the infinite variety of natural appearances which had been unnoticed by the poets of any age or country, so far as I was acquainted with them; and I made a resolution to supply, in some degree, the deficiency. I could not have been at that time above fourteen years of age.

Wordsworth is looking back nearly sixty years (the Fenwick note was dictated in 1843), yet he remembers the very spot, between Hawkshead and Ambleside, where the outline of the oak against the evening sky first struck him. His acquaintance with the work of other writers cannot have been extensive at the age of fourteen, but his resolution is significant: to supply, in some degree, what so many poets had either failed to noticed or failed to find words for – 'the infinite variety of natural appearances'.

An Evening Walk goes some way towards doing this, for what it offers, in almost unreadable profusion, is sharply observed detail. Interspersed through the descriptive writing are passages of moral comment, and in this as so much else the poem belongs unmistakably to the eighteenth century. Thought and feeling are shaped by the logic of the couplet. But of feeling there is remarkably little. For the most part the appeal of *An Evening Walk* is incessantly to the eye: specifically to an eye trained, as so many had been trained by Gilpin and others, to enjoy the picturesque – cloudscapes, effects of light on water or the boles of trees, thickets chequered with the shadows of rose and poppy.

In the same year, indeed the same month, as *An Evening Walk* (January 1793) Wordsworth published his *Descriptive Sketches of the Alps*: a poem nearly twice as long, again in heroic couplets, based on the walking tour with Robert Jones which he comes back to in Book VI of *The Prelude*. The writing is still for the most part objective, but emotion has a larger place. For this, Wordsworth explains, there is a good reason. He had first, he says, given these sketches the title of Picturesque, but that term would be an insult. The Alps are not picturesque, they are sublime: not just appealing to the eye, but awakening awe in the most impassive spectator.

The note I have just paraphrased was provided by Wordsworth for these lines in the first edition of *Descriptive Sketches*:

> Behind his sail the peasant strives to shun
> The west that burns like one dilated sun,
> Where in a mighty crucible expire
> The mountains, glowing hot, like coals of fire.
>
> (1793, 344–7)

This is almost glaringly vivid, and Wordsworth felt the passage needed a further defence:

> Had I wished to make a picture of this scene I had thrown much less light into it. But I consulted nature and my feelings. The ideas excited by the stormy sunset I am

here describing owed their sublimity to that deluge of
light, or rather of fire, in which nature had wrapped the
immense forms around me [that is, the mountains]; any
intrusion of shade, by destroying the unity of the
impression, had necessarily diminished its grandeur.

There are several points of interest here, but chiefly one.
Wordsworth has not, either deliberately or unconsciously,
heightened the scene: it really was as spectacular as he says
it was. Had he wished to make a picture – probably he means
a painting, but it could be in words – he would have 'thrown
much less light into it', for the picturesque depends on the
interplay of light and shade. But the Alps are not picturesque,
they are sublime. To respond to them passionately is right.
Hence 'I consulted nature and my feelings': that is, while he
described the sunset as it really was (a deluge of light, or
rather of fire), his aim was not simply to describe. It was to
recreate in words 'the unity of the impression'. The metaphor
of the crucible, which his mind supplied, was not something
added to make the scene more dramatic. Probably it occurred
to Wordsworth quite spontaneously. At any rate, it captures
something essential in the experience: the fierce splendour of
the sunset and Wordsworth's response to it. Yet Wordsworth, when he wrote these couplets, did not simply consult
his feelings. He consulted nature and his feelings. What he
gives us is not just a surge of excitement, but a scene of
almost hectic brilliance. We may not care for such sunsets,
but that is another matter.

Wordsworth takes up this question of the balance between
nature and feeling (the mind) more than once in *The Prelude*.
In Book XI he explicitly rejects not only the cult of the
picturesque, which was already going out of fashion by the
early 1800s, but any approach to nature which limits itself to
form, colour, subtleties of light and shade. For a while, he
recalls – he is thinking of the summer of 1793, when he first
saw Tintern Abbey and the Wye valley – he delighted in such
things:

> Pampering myself with meagre novelties
> Of colour and proportion, to the moods

> Of Nature, and the spirit of the place,
> Less sensible.   (XI.160)

The tone of these lines has to be read in the context of
Wordsworth's argument: that his imagination, only true to
itself when responding with love to 'the spirit of the place',
was impaired by a period of subservience to the despotism
of the eye. Wordsworth, especially in the early books of *The
Prelude*, is wonderfully alert to 'the trembling lake', gleams of
moonlight on the sea, and so on. But in *The Prelude* these
details are integrated in a larger response, a deep sensitivity
to wood and mountain, clouds, wind and sky. The point of
the whole passage in Book XI (137–94) is that to see nature as
landscape is not enough. A healthy relationship between the
mind and the natural world is not just aesthetic but spiritual:
a response from the heart, not a detached appreciation,
however keenly perceptive, by the eye.

In the Preface to *Lyrical Ballads* Wordsworth writes: 'I have
at all times endeavoured to look steadily at my subject,
consequently, I hope that there is in these poems little
falsehood of description.' This is true – and one reason,
though not the most important, for the success of 'Michael'.
None the less, Wordsworth never cultivated, after 1793, the
eye for detail in nature which he evidently had in youth.
There is rarely any inaccuracy in his writing, but his poetry
by no means excels at describing that 'infinite variety of
natural appearances' which he resolved, before he was fif-
teen, to get into his work. The bareness, even bleakness, of
some of his greatest poetry comes from his refusal to record
more than the simplest elements in a scene – a naked pool,
a broken wall or thorn tree, a rock or cairn. And the austerity
of such writing is not just verbal. It is a moral austerity, an
austerity of vision and feeling.

V

Five years after the appearance of *An Evening Walk* and
Descriptive Sketches of the Alps Wordsworth started to expand
'The Ruined Cottage', begun in 1797, with an account of the
boyhood and youth of its narrator, the Pedlar. The original
poem told the story of Margaret: how poverty drove her

husband Robert to enlist in a regiment that was soon drafted
overseas; how she waited year after year for news that never
came; how cottage and garden fell into neglect, as wind and
rain destroyed the work of human hands; and how she finally
lost all hope and died. The observation is careful and sensitive, but at no point in 'The Ruined Cottage' is there any
suggestion that nature 'liveth to the heart' or that there is One
Life within us and abroad.

The contrast with 'The Pedlar' could hardly be more
marked. In 'The Pedlar' the writing is often passionately
subjective:

> He was only then
> Contented when with bliss ineffable
> He felt the sentiment of being spread
> O'er all that moves, and all that seemeth still,
> O'er all which, lost beyond the reach of thought
> And human knowledge, to the human eye
> Invisible, yet liveth to the heart;
> O'er all that leaps, and runs, and shouts, and sings,
> Or beats the gladsome air; o'er all that glides
> Beneath the wave, yea, in the wave itself,
> And mighty depth of waters.   ('The Pedlar' 206–16)

When Wordsworth took this passage over for *The Prelude*, he
hedged it, as we saw, with doubts and qualifications.
Perhaps he had come to mistrust such enthusiasm, to feel
that the relation between his spirit and the world should be
calmer, more stable. The egotism which struck so many of
his contemporaries (not just Keats) was complex. Partly it
was a matter of temperament, partly a confidence in his own
vocation – a confidence fortified by the attacks of the reviewers.
But the egotism also served as a defence against the eagerness of his spirit to go out of itself, a defence of his own
identity against a world that threatened to absorb it.

This is evident, I think, in Wordsworth's very cautious use
of metaphor. Metaphor is the life of poetry, but metaphor is
a way of seeing and feeling, not a trope of rhetoric. It springs,
as Aristotle said, from an intuitive perception of similarity in
dissimilars, and this may well be what Wordsworth has in

mind when he speaks in *The Prelude* of a habit he had formed,
by the age of seventeen, of looking for

> affinities
> In objects where no brotherhood exists
> To common minds.   (II.403)

The 1850 text ('To passive minds') makes his meaning clearer,
as well as less patronising. Metaphors are created, not just
found, and they are created by that 'kindled state of consciousness' which we call, as Wordsworth and Coleridge
called it, the imagination.[11]

For the 1802 edition of *Lyrical Ballads* Wordsworth wrote
into the Preface a long passage (about three thousand words)
which explores the question 'What is a poet?' When a poet's
subject is well chosen, Wordsworth suggests, it will naturally
lead him to 'passions the language of which, if selected truly
and judiciously, must necessarily be dignified and variegated,
and alive with metaphors and figures'. In general, no doubt,
this is true. Yet a language alive with metaphors and figures
is hardly what comes to mind when we think of Wordsworth.
The simplicity which is often the strength of his writing owes
as much to the very sparing use of metaphor as to Wordsworth's preference for a style almost bare of adjectives. In *The
Prelude*, though there are fine metaphors here and there,
simile is much more common. This is true of most of Wordsworth's poetry, and for a reason: simile allows the poet to
keep a certain distance. Affinities are affirmed, even cele-
brated, but affirmed by a mind that stays outside, not
identifying (as it does in metaphor) with the objects it
responds to.

Wordsworth, in other words, is a poet for whom the
impulse to empathy seems to have represented a threat to the
integrity of the self. Keats, in one of his letters to Bailey (22
November 1817) writes: 'If a sparrow come before my win-
dow I take part in its existence and pick about the gravel.'
This is empathy. Keats is not projecting his own feelings onto
the bird, he is taking part in its life. The richness, though
sometimes also the sluggishness, of his poetry flows from his
readiness to identify in this way with objects outside himself.

In a letter written the same day to Reynolds he quotes the wonderful lines about the snail from *Venus and Adonis*:

> Or as the snail, whose tender horns being hit,
>   Shrinks backwards in his shelly cave with pain,
> And there all smothered up in shade doth sit,
>   Long after fearing to creep forth again.

And in a letter of the following year (27 October 1818) to Woodhouse he aligns himself with Shakespeare rather than Wordsworth:

> As to the poetical character itself (I mean that sort of which, if I am any thing, I am a member: that sort distinguished from the Wordsworthian or egotistical sublime, which is a thing per se and stands alone) it is not itself – it has no self – it is everything and nothing – it has no character.

Shakespeare, for Keats, was the antithesis of the Wordsworthian or egotistical sublime. For Shakespeare, above all, was able to forget himself, to enter with equal sympathy and conviction an Iago or an Imogen (or a snail). A poet, Keats adds, 'has no identity – he is continually in for [informing?] – and filling some other body.'

Empathy is common in Romantic and post-Romantic poetry. It is not, as Keats recognised, characteristic of Wordsworth. Yet 'The Pedlar' suggests that a capacity for empathy, for 'informing and filling some other body' was one Wordsworth as a young poet knew well. Even in his mature work it emerges occasionally, in 'I wandered lonely as a cloud', in the 'trampling waves' of 'Peele Castle', in the great comparison of the Leech-gatherer (a simile, but a simile with the depth and energy of metaphor) to something between a huge boulder and a sea-beast.

In the Simplon Pass (*Prelude* VI.553–72) empathy finds itself in dramatic tension with an opposing impulse. On the one hand Wordsworth is identifying imaginatively with the scene, on the other projecting onto it the turmoil of his feelings:

> The brook and road
> Were fellow-travellers in this gloomy pass,

And with them did we journey several hours
At a slow step. The immeasurable height
Of woods decaying, never to be decayed,
The stationary blasts of waterfalls,
And everywhere along the hollow rent
Winds thwarting winds, bewildered and forlorn,
The torrents shooting from the clear blue sky,
The rocks that muttered close upon our ears –
Black drizzling crags that spake by the wayside
As if a voice were in them – the sick sight
And giddy prospect of the raving stream,
The unfettered clouds and region of the heavens,
Tumult and peace, the darkness and the light,
Were all like workings of one mind, the features
Of the same face, blossoms upon one tree,
Characters of the great apocalypse,
The types and symbols of eternity,
Of first, and last, and midst, and without end.   (VI.553)

The spirit is exalted and shaken, the flesh intimidated, the mind baffled. Peace and tumult, light and darkness, not alternating but heightening each other, are intelligible, if at all, only as the expression of forces invisible to us, of which woods, clouds, rock and cataract, are only symbols.

James Smith, in a fine analysis, asks whether this reaching for a metaphysical explanation is anything more than a desperate attempt to bring nature within the grasp of the human mind: to claim that there must be some ground of being, some first and final cause of a phenomenal world so alien and overwhelmingly beyond us.[12] Yet whatever misgivings we feel (I share Smith's scepticism about the last few lines), the passage as a whole has extraordinary power. From the beginning there is a sense of danger, the risk that at any moment mind and body may lose their balance, and this sense is everywhere heightened by the animism of the writing: from the magnificent 'stationary blasts' of waterfalls, through the 'Winds thwarting winds, bewildered and forlorn' to the muttering rocks, the crags that 'spake by the wayside' and the 'raving stream'. The poetic imagination, Coleridge observed, reveals itself in 'a more than usual state

of emotion, with more than usual order'.[13] The emotion is
there in the driving rhythm and the vividness of word and
phrase, the order in the steady control of syntax – even for
Wordsworth a sentence of seventeen lines is something of an
achievement – and the firmness of the metre.

VI

Blank verse is the most flexible of English metres. The
measure is a line of ten syllables, usually with four stresses
but often five and occasionally three. The iambic pulse which
gives the rhythm its momentum may be faint, emphatic or
irregular. Elisions and slurs make possible a line that has the
sweep of an alexandrine – 'The unfettered clouds and region
of the heavens' – though the twelve syllables are still (at least
arguably) only ten. Above all, the blank verse paragraph,
almost more important than the line for Wordsworth, admits
every variation of speed and pause in response to the
pressure of feeling.

Wordsworth's first published poems were in heroic
couplets, and the sensibility of *An Evening Walk*, though it
chafes a little against the symmetry of the couplet, adapts
itself to the neatness of the form. A 'Tintern Abbey' in couplets
is inconceivable. Even the blank verse of Milton would have
been useless for what Wordsworth now had to say. There are
reminiscences of *Paradise Lost* in *The Prelude*, some of them
deliberate, others apparently unconscious, but the overall
impression we take from the poem, at any rate in its 1805
form – the 1850 text has far more Miltonic emphases and
distortions – is of a writer very different from Milton. Wordsworth's syntax, for example, is rarely periodic. Like Milton
he runs on the sense from line to line, but he has a marked
preference for co-ordinate rather than subordinate clauses:
his favourite conjunctions are the simplest, chiefly 'and', 'or',
'then'. The span of a characteristic paragraph – the Boy of
Winander, say, or even the Simplon Pass – is required not (as
in Milton) to marshal the details of a scene or the divisions
of an argument, but to follow the track of thought as it
responds to different moods. Milton's style is an astonishing
achievement: a high style, as his subject demanded, but even
at its most expressive rarely the voice of a man speaking to

men, or of a man speaking to himself. What Milton valued
in man was not his capacity for feeling but his capacity for
moral choice. If man was made in God's image it is the
rational soul, not the creative sensibility, that reminds us of
the fact and the obligations it implies.

Wordsworth's blank verse owes more to Cowper and
Coleridge – the Coleridge of the conversation poems who
himself had learned from the informality of Cowper. What
both poets admired in *The Task* was the honesty of the
speaking voice, the freedom (or comparative freedom) from
archaism and artifice. Wordsworth, indeed, seldom comes
closer to the idiom of everyday speech than Cowper. Where
he surpasses Cowper is in strength and subtlety of emotion,
and therefore of rhythm.

It was Coleridge who saw how far Cowper's example could
be carried. Wordsworth had written fine blank verse before
the summer of 1798. He had written nothing quite like 'Tintern
Abbey'. Coleridge had. Even before their first meeting he had
composed 'The Eolian Harp'. In 1797–98, when they were
neighbours below the Quantocks – Alfoxden is three or four
miles from Nether Stowey, but three or four miles was
nothing to Wordsworth or Coleridge – he added 'This Lime-
Tree Bower', 'Frost at Midnight' and 'The Nightingale'. The
debt of 'Tintern Abbey' to 'Frost at Midnight' can be exag-
gerated. Wordsworth's poem has depths and shadows, as
well as a breadth of vision, that are not there in Coleridge's.
Still, the debt is not just structural. 'Frost at Midnight'
showed how close it was possible to come to the mobility of
consciousness: to the interplay of thought, never for long
becoming abstract, and feeling.

This is not to say that the mind, as Wordsworth sometimes
suggests, is simply a river. What appealed to him about that
metaphor (he returns to it three or four times in *The Prelude*)
is the way it follows the movement of the mind through time:
travelling forwards, though never in a straight line, often
turning back on itself, always changing, always carrying with
it its own past. But if the image is apt for the life of the mind,
the stream of consciousness with memories occasionally
surfacing from the unconscious, nevertheless the stream will
have to be guided – checked at one place, cleared or deepened

at another – if the result is to be a poem. All good poetry may be, as Wordsworth said, the spontaneous overflow of powerful feelings. (So also, he might have added, is most bad poetry.) But good poetry and a good poem are not quite the same thing. Neither 'Frost at Midnight' nor 'Tintern Abbey' is just an effusion.

The scale of *The Prelude* raised problems of its own. Traditionally, a poem of several thousand lines would be epic, a narrative of heroic action. Wordsworth turns over possible topics in his preamble (I.157–228) and finds he can get no grip on any of them. What he really wants to write is not a poem of events at all, but

> some philosophic song
> Of truth that cherishes our daily life,
> With meditations passionate from deep
> Recesses in man's heart.   (I.230)

The Prelude, of course, is not that poem. This was Wordsworth's, if not quite Coleridge's, conception of *The Recluse* – the great work for which *The Prelude* was to free his powers. When Coleridge, in the early months of 1798, suggested a long poem on nature, man and society, his hope was that Wordsworth, clearing away 'the sandy sophisms of Locke', would be ready to 'deliver upon authority a system of philosophy'.[14] Whether Wordsworth ever saw the project in that light is very doubtful. He had little confidence in analytic thinking, and certainly *The Excursion*, the only part of *The Recluse* to be completed, attempts nothing so ambitious.

The Prelude, though it raises questions often argued in philosophy, makes even less pretence of being systematic. Its structure is not logical but narrative, tracking back to earlier scenes, slowing or turning aside for meditation and description, then gathering itself together to move forward again. Much of its strength lies in its closeness to the dilemmas of experience, and neither in his feeling for the One Life nor in his brooding over the problems of perception could Wordsworth in the years 1804–5, when most of the poem was written, see that experience in the perspective it had for him in the winter of 1798/9. *The Prelude*, therefore, with its

sudden insights, its ambiguities and contradictions, is a poem
to drive the professional philosopher to despair.

On one point, however, Wordsworth is consistent: in all
its traffic with the world the mind is active, or as Wordsworth
prefers to say, creative. The infant babe's ability to unify
objects by the strength of feeling is for Wordsworth 'the first /
Poetic spirit of our human life' (II.275). The babe, that is,
though quite unconsciously, is a maker (*poiein*, the Greek
verb, means to make). What the child is making is the world
in which he will live. He does this by exerting what Coleridge
would later call the primary imagination, and this is a creative
act.

The world 'creative' had a special value for Wordsworth,
assuring him of a continuity beween childhood feeling and
his mature imagination as a poet. In the later years of
boyhood, he says,

> let this at least
> Be not forgotten, that I still retained
> My first creative sensibility,   (II.377)

and in Book XI, reflecting thankfully on his recovery from the
'degradation' of a merely sensuous response to nature (in
1793), he records:

> I shook the habit off
> Entirely and for ever, and again
> In Nature's presence stood, as I stand now,
> A sensitive, and a *creative* soul.   (XI.253)

Coleridge, in Chapter XIII of *Biographia Literaria*, distinguishes carefully between the primary imagination – which
is 'the living power and prime agent of all human perception', as we saw with the infant babe – and the secondary or
poetic imagination, which creates metaphors and plays so
large a part in the shaping of whole poems and other works
of art.[15] Wordsworth in the main might have endorsed this.
But Wordsworth felt no need, as Coleridge did, to ground his
account of the poetic imagination in a fully worked-out
theory of the mind. And for Wordsworth the infant sensibility which organises sensations into perceptions (Coleridge's
primary imagination) shades into the equally creative sen-

sibility which projects its moods and feelings onto the outside world. In *The Prelude*, therefore, perception and imagination are intimately related, and the word 'imagination' silently adapts itself to different contexts. The last few pages of this discussion, in fact, have taken us well into the subject of the next chapter.

3

Imagination

> There are few words in the English language which are
> employed in a more loose and uncircumscribed sense than
> those of the fancy and the imagination.
>
> Addison

The evolution of *The Prelude* from the early drafts written at
Goslar in the winter of 1798/9 to the thirteen books finished
at Grasmere in May 1805 was complex and interrupted. At
what point did Wordsworth decide that his central topic was
the growth of his own mind and specifically his imagination?

As late as January 1804, in a paragraph added at the close
of Book I, he tells Coleridge that his theme is 'the story of my
life' – a larger, less coherent subject. In correspondence too
he refers to the work in this way. At the beginning of March
1804, when he envisaged *The Prelude* as a poem in five books,
of which he had completed four, he speaks of it in a letter to
Hazlitt as 'the poem on my own life'. By December, however,
he was finishing Book X. The phrase has now become (in a
letter to Sir George Beaumont) 'a poem . . . on my earlier life,
or the growth of my own mind'. No doubt this had always
been Wordsworth's chief concern. Books XI and XII are
devoted to the crisis years 1793–96, when his imagination was
'impaired and restored', and the final book, written in April/
May 1805, reminds us that Imagination has been 'our theme'
(XIII.185) all along.

Wordsworth's development of this theme is not easy to
follow. For one thing, he frequently allows it to drop out of
sight for hundreds of lines while he takes up one of his other
themes. For another, 'imagination' is a word with many
facets. Wordsworth uses it more than a dozen times in *The
Prelude*, and different meanings catch the light in different
contexts. Moreover, there are several key passages – the
meeting with the discharged soldier in Book IV, for example
– which are clearly relevant to the growth of his imagination

but where he prefers not to use the word or finds no occasion to do so. And towards the close of the poem, after the ascent of Snowdon, the claims made for the imagination are so extravagant that it is difficult to relate them to Wordsworth's earlier uses of the term.

That said, a rough sketch map of the ground to be covered in this chapter may be helpful. In *The Prelude* Wordsworth seems to think of the imagination chiefly in three ways: as a creative response to landscape, as an intuitive sympathy with men and women, and as one of the powers requisite for the writing of poetry. The connection between these apparently disparate meanings should become clearer as we explore them.

I

On 26 June 1791 Dorothy Wordsworth wrote to her friend Jane Pollard:

> William has a great attachment to poetry . . . which is not the most likely thing to produce his advancement in the world; his pleasures are chiefly of the imagination, he is never so happy as when in a beautiful country.

This use of the term 'imagination' to refer to the appreciation of landscape was by no means new. Addison had explained, in the first of a series of papers in *The Spectator*, that by the pleasures of the imagination 'I mean only such pleasures as arise originally from sight'. He divides these into two kinds: those pleasures 'which entirely proceed from such objects as are before our eyes' and those which are called up in our memory by poems or works of art.[1] Akenside's *Pleasures of the Imagination* makes the same distinction:

> The pleasures of the imagination proceed either from natural objects, as from a flourishing grove, a clear and murmuring fountain, a calm sea by moonlight; or from works of art, such as a noble edifice, a musical tune, a statue, a picture, a poem.[2]

Akenside died in 1770, the year Wordsworth was born. A new edition of his poem came out in 1795. Wordsworth knew it well. (The editor, Lucy Barbauld, herself a poet, was one of the few people to be sent a complimentary copy of the second edition of *Lyrical Ballads*.) Akenside's first book treats

in a rather abstract way of the beauty of natural objects. His
fourth and last book, of which he wrote only a fragment, was
to consider taste as formed by the affections, education, and
the association of ideas. More particularly, it was to look at
the imagination of men of genius: men 'whose imagination
is endowed with powers, and susceptible of pleasures, which
the generality of mankind never participate.'[3] The democrat
in Wordsworth may have flinched a little from the last
phrase, but a passage near the beginning of this fourth book
must have caught his eye:

> O ye Northumbrian shades, which overlook
> The rocky pavement and the mossy falls
> Of solitary Wensbeck's limpid stream;
> How gladly I recall your well-known seats
> Beloved of old, and that delightful time
> When all alone, for many a summer's day,
> I wander'd through your calm recesses, led
> In silence by some powerful hand unseen.
> Nor will I e'er forget you, nor shall e'er
> The graver tasks of manhood, or the advice
> Of vulgar wisdom, move me to disclaim
> Those studies which possess'd me in the dawn
> Of life, and fix'd the colour of my mind
> For every future year.[4]

The verse has an expressiveness, a joy in the recovery of
boyhood scenes and affections, quite unusual for Akenside.
The fact that the poem breaks off soon after this may have
suggested to Wordsworth that here was something still to be
done and well worth doing. At all events, *The Prelude* takes
up Akenside's theme: the poetic imagination and its debt to
the beauty of the natural world.

Wordsworth's poem opens gratefully:

> Oh there is blessing in this gentle breeze,
> That blows from the green fields and from the clouds
> And from the sky; it beats against my cheek,
> And seems half conscious of the joy it gives.   (I.1)

Wordsworth himself breathes more freely – 'Trances of

thought and mountings of the mind / Come fast upon me'
(I.20) – and what he feels is more than relief from the
constraints of the city. It is a delighted renewal of his energies
as a poet:

> For I, methought, while the sweet breath of heaven
> Was blowing on my body, felt within
> A corresponding mild creative breeze,
> A vital breeze which travelled gently on
> O'er things which it had made, and is become
> A tempest, a redundant energy,
> Vexing its own creation.   (I.41)

What this inner, metaphorical (but not just metaphorical)
breeze is, Wordsworth does not need to tell us: the idea of
poetry as inspiration, of the poet/prophet breathed into by
the god (the Latin *spiritus* means both wind and breath, as
well as soul) goes back to Plato. What Wordsworth intends
by 'vexing its own creation' is less clear. Are the 'things
which it has made' fragments of verse which the rising
creative breeze, now a tempest of feeling, throws into confusion? Perhaps.

In this mood, at any rate, poetry comes easily. The real
wind, blowing across the fields and hills, exhilarates him. So
exultant a mood can hardly last, but at sunset there is a brief
recurrence of inspiration:

> It was a splendid evening, and my soul
> Did once again make trial of the strength
> Restored to her afresh; nor did she want
> Eolian visitations.   (I.101)

Characteristically, though no doubt unconsciously, Wordsworth's phrase 'make trial of the strength / Restored to her'
counters any implication that the soul is merely passive. Yet
the image of the Eolian harp is significant. Primarily, of course,
it carries the idea that the imagination is an instrument rather
than a conscious agent: poetry is not so much an art as a
spontaneous overflow of powerful feelings. But at the same
time, since it is to the wind that the harp responds, there is
a suggestion that what prompts the imagination to poetry is

not the activity of men in cities but the life of the natural
world.

Perhaps this is to take the image too literally, yet Wordsworth certainly felt there to be a deep connection between
nature and the imagination. In Book V of *The Prelude* he tells
us that the youth who has been intimate with woods and
fields from boyhood will delight more than others in the
Nature he meets with in great poetry. For

> Visionary power
> Attends upon the motions of the winds
> Embodied in the mystery of words;
> There darkness makes abode, and all the host
> Of shadowy things do work their changes there
> As in a mansion like their proper home.   (V.619)

A few months after finishing *The Prelude* he wrote a letter
(7 November 1805) to Walter Scott, who had undertaken to
prepare a collected edition of Dryden. Wordsworth admires
Dryden's genius, but will not allow it to be a poetical genius:
'the only qualities I can find in Dryden that are *essentially*
poetical are a certain ardour and impetuosity of mind with an
excellent ear.' He has also, Wordsworth concedes, a com-
mand of language. But to grant this is not to grant Dryden
imagination: 'That his cannot be the language of the imagination must have necessarily followed from this, that there is
not a single image from Nature in the whole body of his
works.' As it happens this is not quite true, though the
exaggeration is a useful one. What is interesting is Wordsworth's argument: ardour and impetuosity of mind, with an
excellent ear, may be poetical, but without images from
nature there can be no 'language of the imagination'.

If this sounds sweeping, it is far from being wildly wrong.
Images from nature are rare in Dryden (they are equally rare
in Donne), yet there does appear to be a connection, if not a
necessary one, between poetry and nature. Chaucer and
Shakespeare, whose central concern is the life of men and
women, crowd their work with references to the natural
world, both in its own right and to express human passions.
The poet, as Wordsworth said, is a man of more than usual
organic sensibility; it would be surprising if he did not delight
in landscape and weather, wind, sea and stars. When he

decided to include the skating episode (*Prelude* I.452–89) in a collected edition of his poems, Wordsworth gave it an elaborate but significant title: *Influence of Natural Objects in Calling Forth and Strengthening the Imagination in Boyhood and Early Youth.* The title would serve for virtually the whole of the first two books of *The Prelude*.

In the text of these first two books the word 'imagination' never occurs. Perhaps this is no more than an accident. Wordsworth is remembering the experiences that moved him deeply as a child, and a child's emotional and imaginative life are almost inseparable. 'Fair seed-time had my soul', he tells us, 'and I grew up / Fostered alike by beauty and by fear' (I.305). Fear was important, not so much in enlarging his capacity for awe, as because nothing more readily wakens and works on the imagination. In three of the four episodes in Book I fear is an element in the boy's excitement:

> On the heights
> Scudding away from snare to snare, I plied
> My anxious visitation, hurrying on,
> Still hurrying, hurrying onward. Moon and stars
> Were shining o'er my head; I was alone,
> And seemed to be a trouble to the peace
> That was among them. Sometimes it befel
> In these night-wanderings, that a strong desire
> O'erpowered my better reason, and the bird
> Which was the captive of another's toils
> Became my prey; and when the deed was done
> I heard among the solitary hills
> Low breathings coming after me, and sounds
> Of undistinguishable motion, steps
> Almost as silent as the turf they trod.   (I.318)

The strength of these first two books is their spontaneity. Aside from a few short linking passages, Wordsworth recreates the life of the child with astonishingly little comment from the grown man. Even in the paragraph on the infant babe in Book II, where he traces the earliest stirrings of consciousness, he avoids, or at least never uses, the term 'imagination'.

The concept, though not the word, appears for the first time about a hundred lines after the infant babe passage:

> But let this at least
> Be not forgotten, that I still retained
> My first creative sensibility,
> That by the regular action of the world
> My soul was unsubdued. A plastic power
> Abode with me, a forming hand, at times
> Rebellious, acting in a devious mood,
> A local spirit of its own, at war
> With general tendency, but for the most
> Subservient strictly to the external things
> With which it communed. An auxiliar light
> Came from my mind, which on the setting sun
> Bestowed new splendour; the melodious birds,
> The gentle breezes, fountains that ran on
> Murmuring so sweetly in themselves, obeyed
> A like dominion, and the midnight storm
> Grew darker in the presence of my eye.   (II.377)

If we come to this from *Biographia Literaria* we may read too much into the word 'plastic', and 'general tendency' could hardly be more vague. Still, Wordsworth's essential meaning is plain. His mind in boyhood, though for the most part happy to accept and enjoy the world around him, was always liable to intensify it by projecting an 'auxiliar light' on to the sunset or an auxiliar darkness on to the midnight storm. Whether we are meant to approve or smile at this youthful habit is not quite clear. Perhaps both. At any rate, we are evidently to take it as an early sign of a strong imagination.

But a strong imagination brings with it risks and responsibilities. Every good poet has his own vision of the world. How is that vision, often boldly individual, to be reconciled with the world his readers live in? A fool, said Blake, sees not the same tree that a wise man sees. True enough. But if one sees a tree and the other an angel, how are they to understand each other? This is not a question that would have troubled Blake, who did not write for fools, but the problem is rarely so simple. Valéry has a dialogue (*Dialogue de l'Arbre*) between a poet, Tityrus, and a natural philosopher,

Lucretius. The tree they both admire is a beech.[5] They agree about that. Neither is a fool, both are highly intelligent; and the philosopher, as his name suggests, has a good deal of the poet in him. Still, they see the tree differently.

Kant, though he rejected the commonsense belief that our senses report reality as it is, could still assume that the world we live in is a world we all share. Even if time and space are not features of reality but categories of human thinking, at least we construct and live in a common world. Schopenhauer, forty years later, makes no such assumption. 'The world', he says bluntly, 'is my representation.' My representation, not ours. You live in your world, I in mine. No doubt the two overlap, but why should we expect them to coincide?

This may seem a long way from Wordsworth, who read little philosophy and had none of Coleridge's reverence for Kant, but it goes to the heart of Romantic and post-Romantic poetry. Beyond Schopenhauer, and in the spirit of Schopenhauer, comes the adventure of French Symbolism;[6] beyond that, the subjectivism of Rilke and Eliot, the personal mythology of Yeats, and Wallace Stevens' struggle to balance reality with the imagination. It is Wordsworth rather than Blake who stands at the beginning of modern (or modernist) poetry, for if ever there was a poem of the act of the mind it is *The Prelude*.

Given its head, a strong imagination will impose its own version of reality on the world. The solitary (and Wordsworth was a solitary) is particularly exposed to this danger, just as on other occasions he is more likely to find himself at the edge of the abyss of idealism. In the passage I quoted a moment ago from *The Prelude*, the phrase 'obeyed / A like dominion' anticipates the lines about the mind as lord and master which introduce the spots of time in Book XI. We shall be looking at these lines later. But in Book II Wordsworth is careful to insist that for the most part his youthful imagination was 'Subservient strictly to the external things / With which it communed' (II.386–7). If his mind bestowed new splendour on the sunset, he still saw it as a sunset – not as a mortally wounded dragon, or the funeral pyre of Patroclus. The imagination heightens. It does not, or should not, distort.

In Book VIII Wordsworth comes back to this point, when he glances at the immaturity of his early verse. As in Book II, he is thinking of the time before he went up to Cambridge; probably he would be about sixteen. In those days, he tells us, 'that first poetic faculty / Of plain imagination and severe' (VIII.511) was often adulterated by 'A wilfulness of fancy and conceit' (VIII.521). This wilfulness of fancy could appear in two ways. With human beings it would invent and exaggerate, creating fictitious objects for its sympathy (a vagrant woman with her babes, say) or ascribing to disappointed love a woodman's illness which doubtless had more prosaic causes. In relation to landscape the fancy could be equally wayward, seeing 'a sparkling patch of diamond light' on a wet rock in the distance as the entrance to some magic cave or the shield of a knight buried in the nearby wood (VIII.559–86).

Yet even this 'adulterate power' did something, Wordsworth feels, to enlarge his human sympathies. Sometimes the shapes of fancy were 'grafted upon feelings / Of the imagination' (VIII.584–5). And always, to steady him against the ingenuity of fancy he had 'a real solid world / Of images' about him (VIII.604). Gleams of light, with their suggestions of transcendence, always had a strong appeal for Wordsworth ('gleam' is a favourite word with him). To see the wet rock as a patch of 'diamond light' was a feat, though a small one, of the imagination. To interpret it as the entrance to a magic cave was fanciful, but the rock, after all, was still solidly a rock.

II

In Book III Wordsworth is at Cambridge, where 'Imagination slept' (III.260). Yet he had come there, he knew,

> with holy powers
> And faculties, whether to work or feel:
> To apprehend all passions and all moods
> Which time, and place, and season do impress
> Upon the visible universe, and work
> Like changes there by force of my own mind.   (III.83)

To feel is part of the poet's sacred task; but the real work of the imagination, Wordsworth seems to be saying, is to modify or transform the visible universe as weather and season, light and shade, transform it.

In the spring of 1798, on a stormy day on the Quantocks, Wordsworth saw a stunted thorn-tree shaken by the wind – an object he had often passed in fine weather without noticing it. He was strongly moved, partly perhaps by a memory of his own childhood (*Prelude* XI.344–88), and set to work that evening on a poem which he hoped would make the thorn an equally impressive object to his readers.[7] This is not quite working a change on the visible universe, but it suggests the kind of 'force of my own mind' Wordsworth valued.

Imagination, then, will often reveal itself first as a response to landscape. In effect, it is a kind of intensified perception: perception energised by feeling. From nature, says Wordsworth of his adolescence, 'I had received so much that all my thoughts / Were steeped in feeling' (II.417). And even earlier, in an apostrophe to Nature, he recalls how the 'presences' he felt among the woods and hills

> Impressed upon all forms the characters
> Of danger or desire, and thus did make
> The surface of the universal earth
> With triumph, and delight, and hope, and fear,
> Work like a sea.   (I.497)

Poetry is the spontaneous overflow of powerful feelings. And before such feelings overflow in poetry they are likely to be projected, for the most part unconsciously, on to landscape.

This projection of feeling, intensifying the mind's relationship with nature, recurs again and again in *The Prelude*, not only in the scenes of childhood but in Book VI (the Simplon Pass and Lake Como). Wordsworth, though he does not explicitly link it with the imagination, clearly thinks of it as one of the springs of poetry. For what, he asks, in the enlarged (1802) Preface to *Lyrical Ballads*, is a poet? A man speaking to men, to be sure, but a man who feels more readily and deeply. Feels what? Not just joy, grief or terror, but 'the spirit of life that is in him': 'delighting to contemplate similar volitions and passions as manifested in the goings-on of the Universe, and *habitually impelled to create them where he does not find them'* (my italics). So the Pedlar, near the beginning of 'The Ruined Cottage', can remind us that:

> The Poets, in their elegies and songs
> Lamenting the departed, call the groves,
> They call upon the hills and streams to mourn,
> And senseless rocks – nor idly, for they speak
> In these their invocations with a voice
> Obedient to the strong creative power
> Of human passion.

The mind has always known this impulse to call upon the groves and hills to share its grief. Milton, well aware of the convention in which he is working, claims that they do:

> Thee shepherd, thee the woods and desert caves,
> With wild thyme and the gadding vine o'ergrown,
> And all their echoes mourn.   ('Lycidas', 39–41)

What makes Wordsworth's poetry unusual, what is rare in the pastoral tradition, is not just the direct, first-hand experience of nature (Milton and King, as Johnson remarked curtly, had no flocks to batten). It is the animation of nature by 'the strong creative power' of human passion, not only in elegy but in verse that blends description with meditation: and not as a conscious fiction, recognised as such by poet and reader, but as the true voice of feeling.

Feeling, we saw in an earlier chapter, can disturb the mind's relationship with the world. Excited by his own passions, the poet may no longer see so clearly. His writing becomes subjective. Coleridge admired in Wordsworth's poetry, even as early as 1795, 'the fine balance of truth in observing, with the imaginative faculty in modifying, the objects observed'.[8] But how far can the imagination go in modifying the object? Wordsworth never quite asks this question, but he seems to have it in mind in a preface he wrote for the 1815 collection of his poems, and that essay, though not one of his best – it has none of the moral and social passion, and little of the critical insight, of the Preface to *Lyrical Ballads* – is worth looking at here. Written ten years after *The Prelude*, it cannot be taken as a gloss on the poem, but it does throw some light, if not on 'the growth of a poet's mind', at least on Wordsworth's concept of the imagination.

All the great Romantics affirm the value of the imagination, yet each means something slightly different by the word. Modern criticism, following Coleridge and Shelley (and perhaps Keats), often equates it with the power of writing poetry. Wordsworth does not do this. For him the imagination is only one, though indisputably the highest, of the poet's gifts. He begins his 1815 Preface by listing the powers requisite for the production of poetry and explaining the function of each. Here is his list:

> Observation and description
>> Sensibility
> Reflection
>> Imagination and fancy
> Invention
>> Judgement.

Dryden, though he might have been surprised by Wordsworth's order, would probably have thought this reasonable. Blake, of course, thought it absurd.[9]

Wordsworth goes on to speak in some detail of observation, sensibility and imagination. Observation (and description) is the ability 'to observe with accuracy things as they are in themselves, and with fidelity to describe them, unmodified by any passion or feeling existing in the mind of the describer.' If we leave to one side the question begged here – how can we observe 'things as they are in themselves' if our senses half create the world that they perceive? – this is plain enough. Wordsworth values, rightly, the poet's ability to describe the visible world with precision. Still, his regard for this gift is limited, for 'its exercise supposes all the higher qualities of the mind to be passive, and in a state of subjection to external objects.' These higher qualities of the mind include, naturally, the imagination. Apparently they also include sensibility, 'which, the more exquisite it is, the wider will be the range of a poet's perceptions; and the more will he be incited to observe objects, both as they exist in themselves and as re-acted upon by his own mind.' An exquisite sensibility, the kind of delicate awareness of sound, taste and touch, that we find in Keats, is not characteristic of Wordsworth. His strengths lie elsewhere. But the point he wants to make here is clearly right. A 'more than usual organic sensibility' (his phrase in the *Lyrical Ballads* Preface) prompts the poet to a more eager attention to objects, whether modified by his feelings or not.

This brings us to the imagination. Wordsworth makes things awkward for himself in the 1815 Preface by bracketing imagination with fancy and then trying, not very successfully, to distinguish between them.[10] But again his main point is clear: 'imagination' is a subjective term – it deals with objects not as they are, but as they appear to the mind. Wakened to energetic life by the poet's feelings, the imagination represents objects as they seem to him, modified by those feelings. In an Essay Supplementary to the 1815 Preface, Wordsworth adds that this is the true business of poetry: 'to treat of things not as they *are*, but as they *appear*, not as they exist in themselves but as they *seem* to exist to the *senses* and to the *passions*' (Wordsworth's italics).

This distinction between things as they are and things as they appear to the senses and the passions is one of Wordsworth's major preoccupations in *The Prelude*. Perhaps it was only while writing *The Prelude* that he made it reasonably clear to himself. Imagination is perception heightened, energised by feeling. Feeling has unique importance for Wordsworth, because feeling is what gives the mind its power to create. Feeling itself, as with the infant babe, *is* creative. And from the creativity of the mind in perception (the infant babe's construction of a world of objects) to the creativity of the mind in metrical composition is a long but for Wordsworth entirely natural step. Somewhere between the two, though closer to perception, comes the projection of feeling on to the natural world, as in the spots of time.

The spots of time were originally drafted, like the other childhood episodes of *The Prelude*, in the winter of 1798/99. In that draft they are presented quite simply. There are in our existence, says Wordsworth, certain incidents, often from childhood, which come back to us in later life so that

> our minds –
> Especially the imaginative power –
> Are nourished and invisibly repaired.   (1799, I.292)

To illustrate this he recalls two of his earliest memories: the day when, lost on a darkening moor, he saw a woman with a pitcher struggling to make her way against the wind, and the day some years later when he waited anxiously for the horses that would take him home from school at Christmas. The two incidents – the first took place when Wordsworth was only five, the second when he was a boy of thirteen, a week or two before his father's death – gave birth to some of the greatest poetry in *The Prelude*. But the way they are introduced, and therefore the way we approach them, in 1805 is not at all the way Wordsworth introduced them in 1799.[11]

In 1799 these episodes came after the drowned man (now in Book V). In the 1805 *Prelude* the context is quite different. Wordsworth, well into Book XI, has been speaking of his sensuous response to landscape in 1793. That sensuous delight (the 'dizzy raptures' of his first visit to Tintern Abbey) was transient: not just because in boyhood he had loved nature more deeply, but because

> I had felt
> Too forcibly, too early in my life,
> Visitings of imaginative power,
> For this to last: (XI.250)

– that is, for a mere excitement of the senses, however passionate, to last. He sums up firmly:

> I shook the habit off
> Entirely and for ever, and again
> In Nature's presence stood, as I stand now,
> A sensitive, and a *creative* soul.   (XI.253)

This claim, which brings the paragraph to an end, does double duty. On the one hand, it rounds off that phase of his development when nature was 'a transport of the outward sense' (XI.187). On the other, it provides a launching ground for the opening of a new paragraph:

> There are in our existence spots of time
> Which with distinct pre-eminence retain
> A renovating virtue.   (XI.257)

But the key phrase 'imaginative power', which in 1799 introduced the spots of time, has been used up (at line 252). Wordsworth therefore embarks on a rather ponderous explanation (lines 257–78) of why those spots of time are so important. In them, he says,

> We have had deepest feeling that the mind
> Is lord and master, and that outward sense
> Is but the obedient servant of her will.   (XI.270)

This is far more explicit than anything in the 1799 draft. In 1799, certainly, our minds, 'especially the imaginative power', are nourished by the memory of such moments. But why those moments have this power to nourish Wordsworth does not say. And his silence leaves the spots of time stranger and more powerful. The mouldered gibbet and the naked pool on the moor, the woman with her garments vexed and tossed by the wind, the single sheep and the one blasted tree: all these, unexplained in 1799, have something of the mystery of the 'huge and mighty forms' that moved through the boy's dreams after the night with the stolen boat.

In 1805 the spots of time are slotted into Book XI as part of Wordsworth's account of how his imagination was 'impaired and restored'. His argument is that the memory of those moments renewed his confidence in the power of the mind to transform the world around it. But that was not what the experiences had meant to him as a boy. Probably it was not even quite what they meant to him in the winter of 1798/99, when he wrote the poetry that evokes the experiences for us.

Consider the first episode. The setting is a dark common, with a stone cairn on its summit; below the hill, a naked pool and (the only moving thing) a solitary figure:

> A girl who bore a pitcher on her head
> And seemed with difficult steps to force her way
> Against the blowing wind.   (XI.305)

The image is one of elemental simplicity, of human isolation

in a non-human universe. Water (the pool, the pitcher) is
necessary. It is also necessary, as the rhythm of the second
line reminds us, to contend with a nature that cares nothing
for man in order to fetch it. The child, agitated by loneliness
and fear, would be conscious of this only in so far as the girl
with the pitcher, far from offering the possibility of comfort
and reassurance, would bring home to him more vividly his
own solitude in an alien world. But to say this is to say that
Wordsworth's introduction does less than justice to the
power of his own poetry. For surely the value of the incident
for his mature imagination lay in that sense of a mysterious
universe in which man finds himself an exile, rather than in
any evidence it could offer that feeling (the mind) was 'lord
and master'. The mind was not lord and master, though its
fears played a part in creating the 'visionary dreariness' of the
scene. The creative mind and the world exist in a reciprocal
relationship, neither, even when the stress of feeling is
strongest, wholly subjected to the other.

This comes through quite clearly in the second episode:

> 'Twas a day
> Stormy, and rough, and wild, and on the grass
> I sate half sheltered by a naked wall.
> Upon my right hand was a single sheep,
> A whistling hawthorn on my left, and there,
> With those companions at my side, I watched,
> Straining my eyes intensely as the mist
> Gave intermitting prospect of the wood
> And plain beneath.   (XI.355)

No doubt the tension of waiting for the horses made the
scene even more bleak and wild, but just as certainly the
boy's anxiety must have been heightened by the mist, the
bare wall and hawthorn, and the wailing of the wind. The
mind both alters the world it sees and is altered by it.[12]

III

The spots of time in the 1805 *Prelude* differ from the 1799 draft
not only in the primacy given to the mind as lord and master.
Between the two episodes in 1805 we have a completely new,
and very fine, passage.

In 1799 three pedestrian lines link Penrith beacon (the

woman with the pitcher) to the later incident, waiting for the
horses at Christmas. In 1805, after the preamble (XI.257–78)
the sequence divides as follows:

I Penrith beacon	XI.278–315
transition	315–27
Meditation	328–42
transition	342–44
II Waiting for the horses	344–88

The first transition is of small consequence and the second of
none. The crucial link is the meditation, and it is important
to notice that this was composed not in January 1799, when
the two episodes were drafted, but in March 1804.[13] The
passage is complex:

> Oh mystery of man, from what a depth
> Proceed thy honours! I am lost, but see
> In simple childhood something of the base
> On which thy greatness stands – but this I feel,
> That from thyself it is that thou must give,
> Else never canst receive. The days gone by
> Come back upon me from the dawn almost
> Of life; the hiding-places of my power
> Seem open, I approach, and then they close;
> I see by glimpses now, when age comes on
> May scarcely see at all; and I would give
> While yet we may, as far as words can give,
> A substance and a life to what I feel:
> I would enshrine the spirit of the past
> For future restoration.   (XI.328)

The whole of this passage, and especially the five or six
lines at the heart of it ('The days gone by . . . May scarcely
see at all'), is one of the most moving Wordsworth ever
wrote. He was not quite thirty-four years old. Is he already
anticipating the failure of his imagination? It looks like it.
Certainly the lines owe something of their poignancy to our
knowledge that only a few more great poems were to come.

What are these hiding-places of his power, then, that close
as he approaches? Evidently moments in childhood (he has
just recounted one of the most frightening: Penrith beacon)

when his emotions had an intensity that, for him, gave a visionary quality to the landscape. These are the hiding-places of Wordsworth's power for two reasons: first, because they nourish him with a certainty of the strength of his imagination in boyhood, and second, because they provide – or rather, had provided a few years earlier, when the spots of time and other childhood episodes in *The Prelude* were written – both the subject matter and the emotional energy for some of his greatest poetry.

Wordsworth's next two lines may seem quite clear. I'm not sure they are: 'I see by glimpses now, when age comes on / May scarcely see at all' (XI.337). Does he mean that he rarely sees the world now with the intensity he occasionally saw it in childhood? Or that he rarely recalls his childhood now, in 1804 or 1805 (these lines may be as late as April/May 1805), with the clarity it had for him when he drafted the spots of time five or six years earlier?

These two meanings are quite distinct, and to choose between them is not easy. On the whole, the first seems to me more likely. What Wordsworth fears to lose is not the memory of his childhood but those 'visitings of imaginative power' (XI.252) which had been more frequent, or perhaps more intense, in childhood. The word 'visitings' is significant: the imaginative power is quite unpredictable, unexpected in its arrival, never to be depended on. It comes and goes. And when it goes, leaving the poet for days or weeks unvisited, it may never return. Wordsworth in March 1804 was still writing great poetry – he had recently composed the dream of the Arab Quixote and the ascent of Snowdon – but 1803 had been a disappointing year. Even the poetry of January/February 1804 may have seemed to him slight (not in quality but abundance) when he remembered the winter months in Goslar that had given him the spots of time, the Boy of Winander, four of the Lucy poems, 'Nutting', and the child-hood episodes of *Prelude* I.

Two years before this, in March 1802, he had begun an Ode:

There was a time when meadow, grove and stream,
The earth and every common sight

> To me did seem
> Apparelled in celestial light,
> The glory and the freshness of a dream.

'There was a time': when? Probably twenty years ago, though
Wordsworth does not say so. Even now (1802) the earth is still
beautiful: spring has returned, all nature seems to rejoice. Yet
something, Wordsworth knows, has gone, and irretrievably:
'Whither is fled the visionary gleam? / Where is it now, the
glory and the dream?' These two questions are obviously
one, but one that implies others: was the glory a reality or an
illusion? If a reality, why should it ever have been lost? And
when was it lost? Wordsworth could find no answer to these
questions, and the Ode broke off at this point. He completed
it in March 1804, probably a few days before the meditation
('O mystery of man . . .') that links the spots of time in
Prelude XI.[14]

Stanza V of the 'Immortality Ode' – 'Our birth is but a sleep
and a forgetting' – answers all three questions. The splendour
that invested the world was a reality; it was lost because
'when age comes on' we have to lose it; and Wordsworth lost
it, as all men do, gradually.

The freshness of the world of childhood is an experience
most of us have known (Wordsworth thought it universal).[15]
This is not to say that the 'vision splendid' of the 'Ode' can
be equated at all closely with the childhood episodes of *The
Prelude*. In these episodes, especially in Book I, nature often
threatens or disturbs. It is in stanza IX that the 'Ode' comes
closest to the early books of *The Prelude*. Wordsworth is giving
thanks for the fact that memory at least, the memory of 'what
was so fugitive', survives: especially the memory of moments
when the natural world seemed unreal or not the only reality,
moments haunted by

> those obstinate questionings
> Of sense and outward things,
> Fallings from us, vanishings;
> Blank misgivings of a Creature
> Moving about in worlds not realised,
> High instincts before which our mortal nature
> Did tremble like a guilty thing surprised:

Is he thinking of the stolen boat on Ullswater? He is certainly, as the Fenwick note makes clear, remembering that abyss of idealism which he had recalled in *Prelude* II (359–71).[16]

Stanza IX of the 'Ode' and the two stanzas which follow trace a series of moods, by no means all of equal strength, which offer various consolations for the loss with which the poem opened. That opening is echoed by the passionate and touching cry in stanza X:

> What though the radiance that was once so bright
> Be now for ever taken from my sight,
> Though nothing can bring back the hour
> Of splendour in the grass, of glory in the flower.

A few days later, probably, Wordsworth wrote the meditation that links the spots of time in *Prelude* XI. There too the note is one of sadness and loss. But the 'Ode' and the meditation, though so close to each other in mood, say different things (different, not incompatible). What has been lost in the 'Ode' is a radiance that gave the world of childhood a dream-like freshness and beauty. The source of this radiance was not, Wordsworth is convinced, his own mind. In stanza V of the 'Ode' the growing boy has to accept the shadows of adult life gathering round him, 'But he beholds the light and whence it flows, / He sees it in his joy.' If we ask, 'Well: whence does it flow?' the answer can only be 'from God'. The Platonic myth of the pre-existence of the soul is not to be taken literally, but the tone of the whole stanza, though not Christian, is religious. (We need not believe in Plato's myth to believe, as Wordsworth did by 1804, in a God who transcends the world of nature.)[17] At a first reading it seems strange that 'The Youth who daily farther from the East / Must travel' should be 'Nature's priest'. But Wordsworth is not (or not quite) trying to have it both ways. The 'celestial light', though supernatural, irradiated the natural world and made it lovely. To worship nature, therefore, is to worship God.

The meditation in *Prelude* XI speaks of something quite different. Here, as Wordsworth brings together the two spots of time,

> the hiding-places of my power
> Seem open, I approach, and then they close;
> I see by glimpses now, when age comes on
> May scarcely see at all.   (XI.335)

What Wordsworth is losing, and fears to lose, is still the
intensity of childhood vision. But the emphasis now is on
vision, not on the world. There is no suggestion here that the
world of childhood was irradiated with a celestial light. On
the contrary. The scene he has just been remembering (Penrith beacon and the woman with the pitcher) was one of
'visionary dreariness', and what Wordsworth values is not
the scene itself but the renewed evidence the memory of it
has given him of the power of his creative sensibility:

> O mystery of man, from what a depth
> Proceed thy honours! I am lost but see
> In simple childhood something of the base
> On which thy greatness stands – but this I feel,
> That from thyself it is that thou must give,
> Else never canst receive.   (XI.328)

The hiding-places of Wordsworth's power are those moments
of emotional and imaginative energy when he saw nature,
sometimes indeed as lovely, but often as vast, fearful and
mysterious. And the source of *that* vision, he is sure, was his
own mind. We may believe that the source of the celestial
light of the 'Ode' was also Wordsworth's mind: that the 'Ode'
and the meditation are really lamenting a single loss – the
child's keen sensibility both to the beauty of the world (the
'visionary gleam' of the 'Ode') and its terror (the 'visionary
dreariness' of Penrith beacon). But that was not Wordsworth's belief.

By the spring of 1802, when the first four stanzas of the
'Ode' were written, the dream-like freshness and splendour
of the world of childhood had faded. By March 1804, when
the later stanzas and the meditation of *Prelude* XI were
composed, Wordsworth had begun to fear that his imaginative power was failing too. He does not suggest, in the
'Ode', that this failure was inevitable. (The 'Ode' is not
concerned with the imagination.) Yet in some way, he felt,

the vision splendid and his imaginative power were linked.
In stanza VIII of the 'Ode' he warns the child that his soul
will soon

> have her earthly freight
> And custom lie upon thee with a weight
> Heavy as frost, and deep almost as life!

Later in *The Prelude*, speaking of the value of the imagination,
Wordsworth pauses to deplore the tendency, too strong for
most people,

> Of habit to enslave the mind – I mean
> Oppress it by the laws of vulgar sense
> And substitute a universe of death,
> The falsest of all worlds, in place of that
> Which is divine and true.   (XIII.139)

It is not just the fact or fear of growing old, then – 'I see by
glimpses now, when age comes on / May scarcely see at
all' (XI.337) – that links the meditation of *Prelude* XI with the
'Ode'. The celestial light and the imaginative power, though
these are two quite different things – the source of one
(Wordsworth believed) was God, and of the other his own
mind – are likely to fail with age for the same reason: in the
weight of habit and habitual perception, perception with the
bodily eye alone, 'the most despotic of our senses', they have
a common enemy.

IV

Between childhood and age come the years of strength.
Where does an imaginative writer find that strength? To be
specific, how does Wordsworth's imagination when he was
writing 'The Ruined Cottage' and *The Prelude* differ from the
imagination of the child who saw the woman with the
pitcher, and who projected an auxiliar light on to the sunset
or an auxiliar darkness on to the rising storm?

In the first place the man is fully conscious, as the child
was not, of his own mind; and the man, the poet in his late
twenties, can find words for his emotions – not just the
emotions of maturity but those, as he remembers them, of
childhood. (It is one of the triumphs of the first two books of

The Prelude that Wordsworth, while doing this superbly, manages not to interpose his adult consciousness between us and the child's feelings.) No doubt the man's imagination differs from the boy's in many other ways. Wordsworth draws our attention to one: a wider experience of the world, and with that a wider range of feeling. In *The Prelude* this wider experience is enjoyed first at Cambridge (Book III) and explored more fully in Books VII (London) and IX–X (France). A retrospect, Book VIII, takes us back again to boyhood, as Wordsworth seeks how to show how love of nature led him to a love of mankind.

In the early books of *The Prelude* we heard almost nothing of mankind. Wordsworth speaks with affection and gratitude of his mother and Ann Tyson, 'so motherly and good', with whom he boarded at Hawkshead, but one would never guess that he had three brothers – Richard two years older than himself, John and Christopher a few years younger – who boarded with him and went to the same school.[18] In all the important episodes of Books I and II, and in the spots of time, Wordsworth is alone. He enjoyed riding or skating with his friends, but

> Not seldom from the uproar I retired
> Into a silent bay, or sportively
> Glanced sideway, leaving the tumultuous throng
> To cut across the image of a star . . .   (I.474)

When he goes up to Cambridge he is still alone, the company of young men his own age means little to him: 'I was the dreamer, they the dream' (III.28). True, this refers to his first few days there, when everything was new and strange. Later, he tells us, he could enjoy his solitude only in lonely places:

>   if a throng was near
> That way I leaned by nature; for my heart
> Was social and loved idleness and joy.   (III.234)

Even so, the tenor of the paragraph which ends with these lines is that social life still meant far less to him than 'the deep quiet' of his own thoughts. When he sets off for France and the Alps (Book VI) in his last long vacation he doesn't tell us the name of his companion, though they were together on the road for fourteen weeks. For that matter, towards the end of *The Prelude*, when he comes back to the summer of 1791 to speak of the ascent of Snowdon, he doesn't mention that the friend he climbed with was the same Robert Jones who had walked eleven hundred miles with him through France and the Alps the year before.

Cambridge had disappointed Wordsworth. London appalled him. Between his graduation from Cambridge and the summer of 1795 when he settled with Dorothy at Racedown, Wordsworth lived in London at three periods, each of a few months. In *The Prelude* he writes only of the first of these (February–May 1791). The second is implied as a background to Book X, where he speaks of the confusion of his feelings about the Revolution, but for practical purposes what we have of London (Book VII) is the impact of the city on a young man from the country. And what strikes him about the city is not just its size, but the incessant hustle and triviality of it.

One day, as he wanders the crowded streets, the real world breaks through. I quote from the 1850 text, which is more impressive here:

> And once, far-travelled in such mood, beyond
> The reach of common indication, lost
> Amid the moving pageant, I was smitten
> Abruptly with the view (a sight not rare)
> Of a blind beggar, who, with upright face
> Stood, propped against a wall, upon his chest
> Wearing a written paper, to explain
> His story, whence he came, and who he was.
> Caught by the spectacle my mind turned round
> As with the might of waters; an apt type
> This label seemed of the utmost we can know,
> Both of ourselves and of the universe;
> And on the shape of that unmoving man,
> His steadfast face and sightless eyes, I gazed,
> As if admonished from another world. (1850, VII.635)

The beggar is a human being like himself; yet not like himself, for the blind face cannot return his gaze and registers no awareness of Wordsworth's presence. Like those other

solitaries, the discharged soldier of Book IV and the old
Leech-gatherer – they too are 'propped' and move, when
they move at all, only slowly – the man seems to survive
somewhere beyond human feeling, or to have kept of feeling
only the strength to suffer and endure.

Wordsworth is not a tragic poet; he had not enough
interest in action or motive for that. But no poet since *Lear*
has come closer to the stillness at the heart of tragedy. In *The
Borderers* he draws a distinction:

> Action is transitory – a step, a blow,
> The motion of a muscle – this way or that –
> 'Tis done, and in the after-vacancy
> We wonder at ourselves like men betrayed:
> Suffering is permanent, obscure and dark,
> And shares the nature of infinity.
>
> (Act III, lines 1539–44)

With suffering, which is 'permanent', Wordsworth can
identify. What matters in a poem like 'Michael' or 'The
Ruined Cottage' is not the action, the story, but the 'great
and simple affections of our nature' which the story is there
to illustrate. Another poet might have found such a story in
London. To Wordsworth the great city is a show, a spectacle:
dazzling, gigantic, but wholly superficial. The passage on
Bartholomew Fair – a work that lays 'The whole creative
powers of man asleep' (VII.653–5) – is placed near the end of
Book VII to sum it all up: roundabouts, puppet shows,
hurdy-gurdies, kettle drums, dwarfs, waxworks, lights,
uproar and disorder:

> a type not false
> Of what the mighty city is itself
> To all, except a straggler here and there –
> To the whole swarm of its inhabitants.   (VII.696)

London, in short, meant little to Wordsworth. France, on
the other hand, meant a great deal. On his first visit, though
he shared something of the enthusiasm of the crowds
celebrating the anniversary of the fall of the Bastille – 'France
standing on the top of golden hours, / And human nature

seeming born again' (VI.353) – his objective was the Alps, not Paris. The decisive visit to France was the second one, when he lived there for just over a year (November 1791–December 1792) – a year that included his friendship with Beaupuy and the love affair with Annette Vallon. For Wordsworth, Coleridge and other young men of the time, the Revolution was by far the greatest public event of their lives; and Wordsworth, unlike Coleridge, saw something of the Revolution at first hand. His sympathy with its hopes is obvious, and the crisis of his own life was not due just to the separation from Annette. It was also a moral and intellectual crisis, brought on first by the British declaration of war, and then by news of the reign of Terror.

Yet even when he is speaking of France Wordsworth's sympathies are with man rather than men. He was not by temperament a political poet. What drew him to the Revolution was not any theory of society, but the fortitude, generosity and strength that he found in Beaupuy and the people for whom Beaupuy fought.

Wordsworth tells us that he had been prepared for these qualities by his admiration for the shepherds of his boyhood. Book VIII, just before *The Prelude* moves to France for that crucial year in Wordsworth's life, has the title 'Love of Nature leading to Love of Mankind'. Why love of nature should do this is not self-evident, except in so far as the beauty of nature developed in the child a capacity to feel deeply, which might make it likely that he would come to feel for others. This, however, is not what Wordsworth says. What he tells us is that as a boy he was accustomed to see man as a solitary, almost sublime figure – the shepherd climbing through mists and storms or isolated against the radiance of the setting sun:

> Thus was man
> Ennobled outwardly before mine eyes,
> And thus my heart at first was introduced
> To an unconscious love and reverence
> Of human nature.[19]   (VIII.410)

The shepherd's life is naturally solitary, and sheep farming, unlike agriculture, changed slowly in Wordsworth's lifetime, so he could see the shepherd as a simple, almost biblical figure (the biblical associations are strong in 'Michael'), enduring loss and danger for the care of his flock.

'Love of Nature leading to Love of Mankind', then, is a rather misleading summary of Book VIII. What that book shows us is that seeing shepherds in the impressive setting of the Cumbrian mountains encouraged Wordsworth to form an idealised conception of mankind, of what human nature could be.

It was the year in France, and the aftermath of that year, that enlarged and deepened Wordsworth's sympathies. Between 1793 and 1798 the poet of *An Evening Walk* and *Descriptive Sketches of the Alps* became the poet of 'The Ruined Cottage' and *Lyrical Ballads*. The best of these, and especially 'The Ruined Cottage', are among his greatest poetry. The only thing at all like them in *The Prelude* – it is one of the finest passages in the poem, and I want to look at it in a moment – is the meeting with the discharged soldier in Book IV. This is almost the only example in *The Prelude* of what Wordsworth, in his 1815 Preface, calls 'the human or dramatic imagination': the kind of imagination we find everywhere in Shakespeare and Chaucer. Since Wordsworth is not generally credited with much imagination of this kind – for the most part (Keats was right) he is a poet of 'the egotistical sublime' – the passage is worth looking at in detail.

V

The episode of the discharged soldier (IV.361–504) was drafted even earlier than the childhood sequences of *The Prelude*. It belongs to the months January/March 1798, and has obvious affinities with 'The Ruined Cottage' and 'The Old Cumberland Beggar'. Its genesis, in other words, is in those months at Alfoxden that gave birth to the first edition of *Lyrical Ballads*.

Wordsworth, as we saw, had lived in France for twelve months – months that included a passionate love affair and the friendship with Beaupuy. He returned to England in December 1792, haunted by the horror of the September massacres but still full of hope for the Revolution. The British declaration of war dismayed and outraged him. In the same month, February 1793, appeared Godwin's *Political Justice*, an attempt to establish the principles on which society should be based. Its arguments were soon made more persuasive by the suppression of personal liberty in England – the government fearing the contagion of revolutionary ideas. Wordsworth, who knew what Beaupuy was fighting for, or at any rate what he was fighting against (the poverty of the girl with the heifer: *Prelude* IX.511–34), met Godwin several times, and for a year or two shared Godwin's faith that reason is, or should be, the only criterion of our moral life and therefore of a just society.

The Terror shattered that faith, and left Wordsworth 'endlessly perplexed'. The despair he records in *The Prelude* (X.888–904, XI.1–7) probably dates from the spring and summer of 1796. That winter, when *The Borderers* was written, saw the beginning of his recovery. The spots of time and no doubt other memories of childhood were important, so also were the companionship of Dorothy and the encouragement of Coleridge. In Book XII of *The Prelude*, after speaking of the healing power of nature and memory, Wordsworth tells us how meetings with simple people, often vagrants encountered on lonely roads, restored his trust not in reason but the human heart, in 'men as they are men within themselves' (XII.225):

> 'Of these', said I, 'shall be my song. Of these,
> If future years mature me for the task,
> Will I record the praises, making verse
> Deal boldly with substantial things . . .
>   . . . my theme,
> No other than the very heart of man'.   (XII.231)

The result was the poetry of 1797–98: 'The Ruined Cottage', the Discharged Soldier, and poems like 'The Thorn', 'The Old Cumberland Beggar' and 'The Idiot Boy'.

The Discharged Soldier differs from most of these in looking back to an incident of ten years earlier. Placed at the end of Book IV of *The Prelude*, it evidently recalls an encounter not far from Hawkshead during Wordsworth's first summer vacation from Cambridge.

The encounter takes place at night. Wordsworth has been
walking along a moonlit road,

> My body from the stillness drinking in
> A restoration like the calm of sleep,
> But sweeter far.   (IV.386)

All is solitude and peace. Then, quite unexpectedly, a turning
of the road reveals

> an uncouth shape
> So near that, slipping back into the shade
> Of a thick hawthorn, I could mark him well,
> Myself unseen.   (IV.402)

Wordsworth studies him: a man of unusual height, stiff, lean
and upright; his arms long, his hands bare, his mouth
'ghastly' in the moonlight. A soldier, apparently, though his
uniform has faded; motionless and completely alone:

> From his lips meanwhile
> There issued murmuring sounds, as if of pain
> Or of uneasy thought; yet still his form
> Kept the same steadiness, and at his feet
> His shadow lay, and moved not.   (IV.421)

Overcoming his fear, Wordsworth moves forward, speaks to
the man, and learns his story: the soldier had served in the
tropics, has been discharged on his return to England, and is
now making his way home.

The nearest village, visible through the trees, is only a few
hundred yards away, but all its lights are out. Yet the man
must have food and lodging for the night, and Wordsworth
knows of a labourer's cottage behind the wood. They make
their way there:

> As it appeared to me
> He travelled without pain, and I beheld
> With ill-suppressed astonishment his tall
> And ghastly figure moving at my side;
> Nor while we journeyed thus could I forbear
> To question him of what he had endured
> From hardship, battle, or the pestilence.

> He all the while was in demeanour calm,
> Concise in answer. Solemn and sublime
> He might have seemed, but that in all he said
> There was a strange half-absence, and a tone
> Of weakness and indifference, as of one
> Remembering the importance of his theme
> But feeling it no longer.   (IV.465)

So they reach the cottage, where Wordsworth knocks, and
the sick man is taken in:

> And now the soldier touched his hat again
> With his lean hand, and in a voice that seemed
> To speak with a reviving interest,
> Till then unfelt, he thanked me; I returned
> The blessing of the poor unhappy man,
> And so we parted.   (IV.497)

What makes this episode so moving? Chiefly, of course,
that 'uncouth shape': tall, gaunt and calm. Wasted by fever,
the man is evidently exhausted ('from behind / A milestone
propped him'), yet he returns Wordsworth's greeting cour-
teously and responds with 'a quiet uncomplaining voice' to
his concern. If his body has lost its strength, his mind has
not. His tale is soon told, he is 'concise in answer'; and
though grateful for help, he would not have asked for it.

The economy of the narrative is impressive. Wordsworth
tells us that the soldier had served in the tropics, presumably
the West Indies. Why the man enlisted (was he pressed? did
poverty leave him no choice?) we are not told. Nor do we
know anything of his age, where his home is, whether he has
a wife and children, or how long he has been away. It is
possible, of course, that Wordsworth learned none of these
details. An unkind critic might argue that if he had, they
would certainly be in the poem: for no other poet, except
perhaps Hardy, has Wordsworth's determination to keep to
the facts of any story he has been told. It seems to me more
likely that Wordsworth learned a good deal which he has
silently omitted, and that this selection and simplification is
one reason why the poetry has such power.

In many of his poems Wordsworth does clog the narrative

with prosaic detail. Why not here? Not, I think, because reviews of the *Lyrical Ballads* had stung him on this point. He did cut thirty lines from his 1798 draft when revising the Discharged Soldier for inclusion in *The Prelude*, but even the poem of 1798 is remarkably uncluttered.[20] Probably there are two reasons for this. First, the incident stayed in Wordsworth's mind ten years before it turned into a poem. His memory was good, but in ten years some of the accidentals of the meeting would have fallen away, or no longer have seemed worth recording. Second, where his imagination is fully engaged, Wordsworth recognises the essentials of a situation and keeps to them.

In *The Prelude*, I said earlier, the word 'imagination' appears more than a dozen times, and its meaning varies in different contexts. In relation to men and women Wordsworth uses the word to mean the ability of the mind to picture and sympathise with the actions and feelings of other people.[21] Does Wordsworth sympathise with others in this way? Coleridge, who recognised 'a meditative pathos' as one of the excellencies of Wordsworth's poetry, went on to identify that pathos as 'a sympathy with man as man; the sympathy indeed of a contemplator, rather than a fellow-sufferer'.[22] On the first point, Coleridge is surely right: Wordsworth's sympathy goes out to the humanity, not the personality, of his characters. Coleridge's afterthought is more debatable. In conversation he put it more strongly. Wordsworth and Goethe, he observed, though not much alike, share one peculiarity: an 'utter non-sympathy with the subjects of their poetry. They are always, both of them, spectators *ab extra*, – feeling *for*, but never *with*, their characters.'[23] Coleridge is Wordsworth's most perceptive critic, and of many of Wordsworth's poems this comment would be true. It is not, I think, true of 'The Ruined Cottage', 'Michael' or 'The Thorn'; nor is it quite true of the Discharged Soldier.

To be sure, the sympathy is implied rather than stated. The only direct reference to Wordsworth's feeling for the soldier is brief:

> Long time
> Did I peruse him with a mingled sense
> Of fear and sorrow.   (IV.419)

The word 'sorrow' is well chosen: 'pity' would bring us closer to the figure in the moonlight, but would take something from his dignity and strength. The sympathy is 'with man as man', not with an individual but with human pain. But Wordsworth has not yet spoken to the stranger. As the incident unfolds, the tact and understatement of the writing – 'As it appeared to me / He travelled without pain' – give weight to the quiet climax a moment later:

> Solemn and sublime
> He might have seemed, but that in all he said
> There was a strange half-absence, and a tone
> Of weakness and indifference, as of one
> Remembering the importance of his theme
> But feeling it no longer.   (IV.473)

The word 'sublime', immediately qualified, has been earned. Moralising and sentimentality, which so often weaken poetry of this kind – even, at moments, so fine a poem as 'The Ruined Cottage' – are completely absent. Wordsworth is able to offer the soldier practical help, and near the end there is a moment of intimacy: 'Assured that now my comrade would repose / In comfort . . .' (IV.488). In his 1798 draft Wordsworth uses that phrase 'my comrade' again a little later. In revising it for *The Prelude* he wisely reverted to 'the soldier', a phrase that recognises the independence of the other – he is not just an object of charity, or an occasion for Wordsworth to feel glad that he has been able to help – as they separate:

> And now the soldier touched his hat again
> With his lean hand, and in a voice that seemed
> To speak with a reviving interest,
> Till then unfelt, he thanked me.   (IV.497)

As with 'Michael' and 'The Ruined Cottage', the strength of the poetry is its restraint. And as with these, there is a blend of simplicity with an occasional formality of word and phrase that raises the writing above the commonplace: 'He was of stature tall, / A foot above man's common measure tall' (IV.405); and later, 'Nor while we journeyed thus could I forbear / To question him of what he had endured' (IV.469). For the most part Wordsworth's tone is entirely natural, that of 'a man speaking to men'. Yet scattered apparently at random through the episode are words, not indeed unusual, but not common in the spoken language: peruse, specious, salutation, reproof, discourse, and so on. The style, unobtrusively precise, is rarely colloquial.

This is hardly the style a reader of the Preface to *Lyrical Ballads* would expect from Wordsworth. But the *Lyrical Ballads* themselves, or many of them, range farther afield in diction and idiom than the Preface would suggest. The impetus to write poems like 'Old Man Travelling', 'The Thorn' and the Discharged Soldier, came from stresses deep in Wordsworth's personal life, from the need to find a voice for human love and human pain. In the Preface his central concern is to justify his choice of incidents by pointing out that what gives these incidents significance is not the story (which is often slight) but the feeling – 'the essential passions of the heart' – which the story illuminates. His defence of the style of the poems is grounded in this larger, essentially moral, purpose. The *Lyrical Ballads* are to be true to life: not the life of fashionable society, but of shepherds, labourers, beggars and the very poor. This, for Wordsworth, is real life – unaffected, close to nature, and strong. The diction of *Lyrical Ballads*, therefore, will be 'a selection of the real language of men in a state of vivid sensation'. When he speaks in his own person, it is this language that the poet should have in mind. When he identifies with the passions of others, as in a poem like 'The Thorn' or 'The Idiot Boy', the poet will keep as far as he can to their own words. For he will recognise that 'no words, which his fancy or imagination can suggest, will be to be compared with those which are the emanations of reality and truth.'

So strongly did Wordsworth feel about this that his dislike of a vicious rhetoric – the poetic diction of Gray and the late eighteenth century – almost became a mistrust of any rhetoric. Not quite; for every style, even the simplest, has its rhetoric. Like 'The Ruined Cottage' and the best of the *Lyrical Ballads*, the Discharged Soldier draws on something more than a 'selection of the real language of men', even in a state of vivid sensation; but like them, in its very sparing use of metaphor, or figurative language of any kind, it gives very movingly an impression of the real language of men.

VI

The imagination of the mature Wordsworth differs from the excited imagination of the boy not only in the wider range of his human sympathies. Characteristic of Wordsworth after 1798 – *The Prelude* is the supreme example, but there are others – is a tendency to look back, to rely on memory to reawaken feeling and generate poems. Sequence after sequence in the first two books of *The Prelude* shows how strongly the emotions of twenty years earlier could come to life again in Wordsworth's mind. But not all the great poetry in *The Prelude* is of childhood. The meeting with the discharged soldier looks back to his first long vacation from Cambridge, the Simplon Pass to the summer of 1790, the dream of the Arab probably to a year or two later. Finally, if the central theme of *The Prelude* is, as Wordsworth claims, the imagination, the summit of the whole poem is clearly Snowdon. Not that it offers the greatest poetry – there are finer passages in Book I and elsewhere – but in the sense that it presents the most formidable challenge to the reader. If we try to take *The Prelude* as autobiography, the ascent of Snowdon will seem oddly out of place. If, on the other hand, we are following Wordsworth's struggle to understand the imagination, the episode comes, as Wordsworth meant it to, as a climax to everything that has gone before. It opens the last book of the poem, and even when he thought of *The Prelude* as a poem in only five books, this was always the position Wordsworth intended it to have.

The ascent was made, with his friend Robert Jones, in the summer of 1791. They start at night – a warm, close night, with a thick mist. As they near the top the moon emerges overhead and Wordsworth finds himself above 'a huge sea of mist, / Which meek and silent rested at my feet' (XIII.43). On every side hills heave their 'dusky backs', like huge whales, above this ocean of mist, while the mist itself reaches out, in what now seem headlands and promontories, into the real sea (Caernarvon Bay and the Atlantic) far to the west:

> Meanwhile, the moon looked down upon this shew
> In single glory, and we stood, the mist
> Touching our very feet; and from the shore

At distance not the third part of a mile
Was a blue chasm, a fracture in the vapour,
A deep and gloomy breathing-place, through which
Mounted the roar of waters, torrents, streams
Innumerable, roaring with one voice.
The universal spectacle throughout
Was shaped for admiration and delight,
Grand in itself alone, but in that breach
Through which the homeless voice of waters rose,
That dark deep thoroughfare, had Nature lodged
The soul, the imagination of the whole.   (XIII.52)

Wordsworth is at his most obscure. He goes on to a kind
of exegesis (XIII.66–119) which draws a parallel between
nature and the human mind. The parallel is far from easy to
grasp. Part of the difficulty of the whole episode is this: that
Wordsworth offers us at once an example and an emblem, or
rather two emblems, of the modifying power of the imagination. In translating the layers of mist into a 'meek and silent'
ocean, then (almost at once) into capes and headlands reaching
into the real sea, the imagination is at its characteristic work
of transforming the external world. The mist (hiding and
revealing crags and contours) does this in one way, the moon
(shaping and reshaping the scene as its light falls on rock and
gully) in another. Moon and mist are both emblems of the
imagination, but of course the mist, rather confusingly, is
also part of the landscape altered by the moon.

There is a further difficulty. In the 1805 text it is in the blue
chasm, with the homeless voice of waters roaring through the
vapour, that Nature has lodged 'The soul, the imagination of
the whole'. In 1805, in other words, the creative mind appears
to be represented both (in its serene, transforming function)
by the moon and also (in the dynamic energy of its depths)
by the gloomy chasm. Each of these images captures something of the mind's power, but to hold them together as we
read is not easy.[24]

To associate mist with the imagination seems to have been as
natural for Wordsworth as Coleridge found it natural to link
the imagination with moonlight. In Book VIII of *The Prelude*

the first incident Wordsworth brings forward to show how love of nature led him to love of man is a moment of joy in childhood, when the mist and low-lying cloud that had been eddying through the valleys parted to reveal on the hillside above him a shepherd and his dog:

> inhabitants
> Of an aërial island floating on,
> As seemed, with that abode in which they were,
> A little pendant area of grey rocks,
> By the soft wind breathed forward.[25] (VIII.97)

At other times, climbing for ravens' eggs or fishing in one of the lonely streams, he would be 'surprized with vapours' and see a shepherd emerge only a few steps away from him, 'In size a giant, stalking through the fog, / His sheep like Greenland bears' (VIII.401). And in the second of the spots of time (XI.344–88) the scene below the boy appeared and disappeared as the mist 'advanced in such indisputable shapes' along the road he was watching.

Mist can alter mountainous country dramatically. In his notably sober *Guide to the Lakes* (1810), Wordsworth observes that the apparent forms and colours of the mountains 'are perpetually changed by the clouds and vapours which float round them: the effect indeed of mist or haze, in a country of this character, is like that of magic.'[26] In a supplement to the fourth edition (1823) he adapted and amplified an extract from Dorothy's account of an excursion in November 1805. They started from Grasmere and have reached the Kirkstone Pass:

> Near the top of the Pass is the remnant of an old wall, which (magnified, though obscured, by the vapour) might have been taken for a fragment of some monument of ancient grandeur, – yet that same pile of stones we had never before even observed.

So far Dorothy, only slightly improved. Then Wordsworth:

> This situation, it must be allowed, is not favourable to gaiety; but a pleasing hurry of spirits accompanies the surprise occasioned by objects transformed, dilated or

distorted, as they are when seen through such a medium.[27]

Probably it was this habit of associating mist with the transforming power of the mind that suggested the strange image of 'an unfathered vapour' in *Prelude* VI, when Wordsworth turns aside from his sense of anticlimax at learning that 'we had crossed the Alps' with the cry:

> Imagination! – lifting up itself
> Before the eye and progress of my song
> Like an unfathered vapour, here that power,
> In all the might of its endowments, came
> Athwart me. I was lost as in a cloud,
> Halted without a struggle to break through,
> And now, recovering to my soul I say
> 'I recognise thy glory.'   (VI.525)

'Imagination' has nothing to do here with writing poetry. The imagination is that power of the mind which had made the crossing of the Alps appear so daunting, the prospect of it so momentous. And this, Wordsworth recognises, is the glory of the soul – its capacity for the infinite:

> In such strength
> Of usurpation, in such visitings
> Of awful promise, when the light of sense
> Goes out in flashes that have shewn to us
> The invisible world, doth greatness make abode,
> There harbours whether we be young or old.
> Our destiny, our nature, and our home,
> Is with infinitude – and only there . . .   (VI.532)

VII

Book XIII, after the ascent of Snowdon, seems to try too hard. Except where Wordsworth turns to Dorothy or Coleridge, when his tone recovers something of informality and even intimacy, the verse settles into the rhythms of a public lecture. Snowdon, as we saw, was offered as an analogue: mist and moon, in their different ways, remind us of the power of the imagination, its readiness to transform the visible world. This is in line with the account of creative sensibility in Book II (the projection of an auxiliar light onto the sunset) and with the spots of time in Book XI. But Wordsworth is coming towards the close of his poem, and wants to claim more for the imagination. He begins:

> A meditation rose in me that night
> Upon the lonely mountain when the scene
> Had passed away, and it appeared to me
> The perfect image of a mighty mind,
> Of one that feeds upon infinity,
> That is exalted by an under-presence,
> The sense of God, or whatsoe'er is dim
> Or vast in its own being.   (XIII.66)

It takes us a moment or two to realise that by 'a mighty mind' Wordsworth means the mind of man at its strongest and most creative, and the last two lines, though characteristically honest, are disconcerting. Which is it that exalts the mind: a sense of God, or whatever is dim and vast in its own being? In the 1850 text Wordsworth solves his problem by suggesting that these are really the same thing:

> There I beheld the emblem of a mind
> That feeds upon infinity, that broods
> Over the dark abyss, intent to hear
> Its voices issuing forth to silent light
> In one continuous stream.   (1850, XIV.70)

(The allusion is to the opening of *Paradise Lost*, where Milton invokes the Holy Spirit which 'Dove-like satst brooding on the vast abyss / And mad'st it pregnant,' yet which still prefers 'Before all temples th'upright heart and pure'.)

So far, though his phrasing has been rather cryptic, Wordsworth is not saying anything he has not said before. The creativity of the mind, he had told us earlier, is divine or at least godlike (III.171–4, IV.151–61). Now, however, he goes further. After some lines on the transforming power of 'the glorious faculty' (imagination) which higher minds are endowed with, he says of such minds:

> in a world of life they live
> By sensible impressions not enthralled

> But quickened, rouzed, and made thereby more fit
> To hold communion with the invisible world.
> Such minds are truly from the Deity,
> For they are powers.   (XIII.102)

Are other minds, then, not truly from the Deity? And is it really imagination that makes the mind more fit to commune with the invisible world? Perhaps it is, but it is not easy to see how, or even to be sure what Wordsworth means here. The reference to 'a world of life' looks forward to a passage forty lines later, where he deplores the power of habit to enslave the mind:

> I mean
> Oppress it by the laws of vulgar sense
> And substitute a universe of death,
> The falsest of all worlds, in place of that
> Which is divine and true.   (XIII.139)

This sounds like a last re-affirmation of the One Life within us and abroad: a life which, it would now seem, is perceptible only by those who have kept their imagination fresh and strong. But the earlier lines are still puzzling:

> in a world of life they live
> By sensible impressions not enthralled
> But quickened, rouzed, and made thereby more fit
> To hold communion with the invisible world. (XIII.102)

The general sense is clear. When the imagination is alert, we are not 'enthralled' by sense impressions. We see through the eye, as Blake would say, not with it. But what exactly is 'the invisible world' (in 1850 'the spiritual world'): a reality beyond the 'world of life' altogether?

It may be useful to recall the great tribute to the Imagination in Book VI. Generated by the memory of crossing the Alps, that tribute (the 'unfathered vapour' paragraph) was written a few weeks after the lines we are trying to elucidate in Book XIII.[28] At that point in Book VI we meet 'the invisible world' in a different context:

> In such strength
> Of usurpation, in such visitings
> Of awful promise, when the light of sense
> Goes out in flashes that have shewn to us
> The invisible world, doth greatness make abode,
> There harbours whether we be young or old.
> Our destiny, our nature, and our home
> Is with infinitude – and only there;   (VI.532)

Wordsworth's excitement is unmistakable, and the reference to 'infinitude' suggests a reality that transcends the limits of space and time. Our true home, the lines seem to say, is not in this world but another. Yet the emotion of the whole paragraph – I have quoted only the central passage; it runs to more than twenty lines – is not so much religious (though it is partly religious) as humanistic, an exultant awareness of the power of man's mind: 'Strong in itself, and in the access of joy / Which hides it like the overflowing Nile' (VI.547).

At several places in *The Prelude*, often when his mind has been excited by is own energy – the crossing of the Alps, the Simplon Pass, Snowdon – Wordsworth's poetry reaches out towards something ineffable. Words (infinitude, eternity) have still to be used, but they are hardly more than gestures. What they point to is something beyond words and apparently beyond the natural world. To the mystic this inadequacy of language is familiar. But for the true mystic the experience itself, a momentary insight into the eternal, carries absolute conviction. If he cannot tell us what he felt it is because language is at home only in the world of time, not because he has any doubt of what he felt.

Wordsworth had no such confidence. Even in 'Tintern Abbey', where he speaks of 'that serene and blessed mood' when

> with an eye made quiet by the power
> Of harmony and the deep power of joy
> We see into the life of things

he recognises that this may be 'but a vain belief'. In *The Prelude* he is not certain whether such experiences are glimpses of a supernatural reality or simply insights into the unfathomable depths of his own mind. What Wordsworth most deeply valued in his own mind was its creativity, and since these rare moments when 'the light of sense / Goes out' were also, he felt, profoundly important, he sometimes tries to bring the two together. That is, he occasionally claims that it is the imagination which enables us to apprehend 'the invisible world'.

If the imagination is still to be equated with the transforming power of the mind, this is confusing. Both kinds of experience, the mystical insight and the energy of the mind's response to landscape, are mysterious. In both it is the intuitive, not the rational, life of the mind that is engaged. In both the mind goes out of itself, or goes out of its awareness of the body, and finds itself free from the constraints of space and time. The fact remains that mysticism and poetry are two quite different things; that a capacity for the infinite, or at any rate a discontent with the finite, is probably universal, while the mystical experience has always been rare; and that Wordsworth's linking of the imagination in Book VI, and more explicitly in Book XIII, with glimpses of a transcendent reality is difficult to relate to his more limited uses of the word elsewhere.

Of course 'imagination' is a word of many meanings, but in *The Prelude* Wordsworth has thought of it chiefly in three ways: as the creative sensibility that alters a landscape under the stress of strong feeling, as an intuitive sympathy with men and women, and as one of the gifts requisite for the writing of poetry. The Snowdon sequence begins by celebrating the power of the imagination (mist and moon) to transform the visible world, but then glides into a claim that the imagination also gives us access to a reality beyond the visible world altogether.

The truth is that by the time we have reached Book XIII the concept of the imagination is being stretched to cover everything Wordsworth values in the human mind. To those who have fostered their imagination, he says, is given consciousness 'of whom they are'. And 'hence' (hence?) religion, faith, intuition and discursive reason, inner peace, intensity of feeling, cheerfulness, truth in moral judgements, and delight in the external universe (XIII.107–19).

Well, it's an impressive list. We are reminded of Wordsworth's own remark in the Essay Supplementary to his 1815 Preface: 'The word, imagination, has been overstrained from impulses honourable to mankind, to meet the demands of the faculty which is perhaps the noblest of our nature.'

The last few pages of *The Prelude*, then, are a disappointment. The reason for this is not just fatigue, though Wordsworth had been working hard at his poem for more than a year. A far heavier burden was the death of his beloved brother John, drowned at sea in February 1805. For ten weeks after the news reached Grasmere Wordsworth wrote almost nothing. When he took up *The Prelude* again in April it was with a heavy heart, and as a duty to be completed. The ascent of Snowdon had been drafted the year before, but three-quarters of Book XI and the rest of Books XII–XIII were huddled together in something like four weeks.

Any long poem will be very uneven, and to give too much weight to its closing pages would be absurd. Naturally the most imaginative writing in *The Prelude* is not to be found in places where Wordsworth is telling us how important the imagination is. The great poetry, where we need no telling, is the poetry of experience – mostly, not quite all, boyhood experience: more than half of Books I and II; the Discharged Soldier, the dream of the Arab, the Boy of Winander and the drowned man; the Simplon Pass; the blind beggar in London; the two spots of time, especially the first, in Book XI; and the ascent of Snowdon (XIII.1–65). That is, well over a thousand lines in a poem of nearly eight and a half thousand. It is an astonishingly high proportion.

Composition of *The Prelude*

The Prelude was neither planned nor foreseen. Wordsworth had been thinking of something quite different, a long poem on nature, man and society. The idea for this had come from Coleridge, and by March 1798 Wordsworth had a title for it: *The Recluse*.

A title, no plan, but a good deal of material. 'The Ruined Cottage', the story of Margaret (told by the Pedlar), had already grown to a poem of around five hundred lines. In January–March 1798, drawing on his memories of Hawks-head, Wordsworth added a long account of the Pedlar's boyhood and youth. About the same time he composed two other blank verse pieces: 'The Old Cumberland Beggar' and the meeting with the Discharged Soldier (now in *Prelude* IV). None of this material seemed right for *Lyrical Ballads*. Any or all of it might find a place in a poem on so large a theme as Nature, Man and Society.

For the next few months Wordsworth was occupied with shorter poems. 'Tintern Abbey' was composed in July. By September 1798, while *Lyrical Ballads* was going through the press, he and Dorothy were on their way to Germany with Coleridge.

Wordsworth still had no thought of a poem that would review his life up to that time (he was twenty-eight). What he found himself writing in Goslar, as the first drafts and fragments took shape, were passages of anything from a dozen to thirty or forty lines about his childhood. The first connected sequence begins abruptly:

> was it for this
> That one, the fairest of all rivers, loved
> To blend his murmurs with my nurse's song

And from his alder shades and rocky falls
And from his fords and shallows sent a voice
To intertwine my dreams?

Was it for what? Wordsworth does not say, and perhaps was
not sure. The explanation in the 1805 text, the first complete
version of *The Prelude*, is clear enough: Wordsworth has been
meditating a long poem, an epic or 'philosophic song', and
is dismayed to find himself, whether from some imperfection
in his theme or from diffidence of his own powers, unable to
get started. 'Was it for this . . .' might then be paraphrased
as 'Was I given such a privileged childhood, the ideal prep-
aration for the life of a poet, only to prove unworthy of that
vocation now?' But this explanation, indeed virtually the
whole preamble (I.1–271), was an afterthought.[1] At the time,
October or November 1798, Wordsworth simply went on
writing.

When he left Goslar with Dorothy in February 1799 he had
composed more than four hundred lines. These include all
the key episodes in Book I – bird-snaring at night, the raven's
nest on the crags, the stolen boat, skating – together with
several bridge passages. They include also four other scenes
of childhood: the Boy of Winander and the drowned man,
which Wordsworth later moved to Book V, and the two spots
of time which ended up in Book XI.

In the summer and autumn of 1799 Wordsworth and
Dorothy stayed with the Hutchinsons at their farmhouse in
Co. Durham. Here he drafted another five hundred lines –
roughly the present Book II, which takes him up to the age
of seventeen. He now had a poem, untitled, of nearly a
thousand lines, which Dorothy transcribed at the beginning
of December. This is the two-part *Prelude* of 1799. (For some
reason it does not include the Boy of Winander, though that
paragraph had been drafted.)[2] Whether Wordsworth thought
of this MS as complete is not certain. Probably he saw it as a
clearing of the ground, an attempt to understand himself,
before starting *The Recluse* – that project for a great philosophic poem which haunted him for the next thirty years. *The
Recluse*, however, continued to hang fire, and the poem on
his own life (*The Prelude*) lay virtually untouched for four
years.[3]

In December 1803 Coleridge arrived at Grasmere and stayed for three weeks. Wordsworth read him Part II (Book II) of *The Prelude* and it was probably Coleridge's enthusiasm that prompted renewal of work on the poem. Wordsworth may have hoped to finish it before Coleridge left for Malta, for in late January or early February he writes to Francis Wrangham that he is 'engaged in a Poem on my own earlier life which will take five parts or books to complete, three of which are nearly finished'.

This is the first reference to a five-book *Prelude*. The ascent of Snowdon, which was to open the last of the five books, was composed in February 1804. Sometime in March, however, Wordsworth decided to enlarge his scheme to about twelve books, taking in his year in France and his response to the Revolution. With this he went ahead steadily for more than a year, completing the poem in May 1805.

Wordsworth was disappointed with his achievement. He returned to the MS, however, on a number of occasions, making cuts, additions and changes, by no means always for the better. A few months after his death in 1850 the poem, now arranged in fourteen books, was published. The title was supplied by the poet's widow (Mary Hutchinson).

The Prelude, therefore, exists in three versions:

      the 1799 Prelude in two parts
      the 1805 Prelude in XIII books
      the 1850 Prelude in XIV books.

A more detailed account of the poem's evolution will be found in the Norton edition, which prints all three versions and includes a discussion by Jonathan Wordsworth of the 1799 *Prelude*. There is a useful comparison of the 1805 and 1850 versions in the parallel text edition of E. de Selincourt, revised by Helen Darbishire (Oxford, 1959). This comparison appears also in de Selincourt's edition of the 1805 text, revised by Stephen Gill, which is available separately. Photographic reproductions and transcripts of the early MSS are published in *The Prelude, 1798–1799*, ed. Stephen Parrish, Cornell University Press, 1977.

Imagination and Fancy

Fancy is not a word we find much use for now, but it turns up frequently in *The Prelude*, not always clearly distinguished from imagination. Until the end of the eighteenth century the terms were almost interchangeable, though fancy (or 'fantasy' as it often appears in Shakespeare) might be thought of as more playful. Addison, in a series of papers in *The Spectator* (nos. 411–421), make no distinction between the two words and evidently thought of them as synonyms. Johnson, while he acknowledges several meanings – eight for fancy, three for imagination – begins his entries in the *Dictionary* by defining each term in a way that aligns it with the other:

> FANCY: 1. Imagination; the power by which the mind forms to itself images and representations of things, persons, or scenes of being.
>
> IMAGINATION: 1. Fancy; the power of forming ideal pictures; the power of representing things absent to oneself or others.[1]

The two terms, Coleridge explains in Chapter IV of *Biographia Literaria*, derive from the use of the Latin word *imaginatio* to translate the Greek *phantasia*; and a more apposite translation, he concedes, would be hard to think of. Yet as soon as he heard Wordsworth read his own poetry, he recognised 'the union of deep feeling with profound thought; the fine balance of truth in observing with the imaginative faculty in modifying the objects observed.'[2] This excellence 'I no sooner felt than I sought to understand', and he could understand it only by distinguishing imagination from fancy.

Probably he worked out the distinction in conversation with Wordsworth. In 1800, at any rate, Wordsworth added a long note in the second edition of *Lyrical Ballads* to defend his choice of a superstitious old sea captain as narrator of 'The Thorn'. He takes the occasion to discriminate between fancy and imagination:

> Superstitious men are almost always men of slow faculties and deep feelings: their minds are not loose but adhesive; they have a reasonable share of imagination, by which word I mean the faculty which produces impressive effects out of simple elements; but they are utterly destitute of fancy, the power by which pleasure and surprise are excited by sudden varieties of situation and by accumulated imagery.

This does not take us far, but it tells us something: that imagination, stimulated by deep feeling, produces impressive effects out of elements in themselves simple; and that the characteristic of fancy is to excite pleasure and surprise.

In the long insertion written for the Preface to the third (1802) edition of *Lyrical Ballads* Wordsworth uses the two terms less carefully. He is arguing that the poet's language will not differ, except by selection, from the speech of ordinary men and women under stress of personal feeling. For the poet will recognise that 'no words, which his fancy or imagination can suggest, will be to be compared with those which are the emanations of reality and truth.' If fancy and imagination are different faculties, then, Wordsworth seems to feel that the difference is of no great moment in comparison with the poet's obligation to be true to human passion.

By 10 September 1802, in a letter to William Sotheby, Coleridge was fairly clear in his own mind about the matter. Clearer still by 15 January 1804, when he writes in a letter to Richard Sharp that in Wordsworth's poetry he finds 'Imagination, or the *modifying* power in that highest sense of the word, in which I have ventured to oppose it to Fancy, or the *aggregating* power – in that sense in which it is a dim analogue of creation.' Imagination is 'a dim analogue of creation' because it shapes and unifies the objects of experience, while Fancy merely collects and juxtaposes. In an article eight years later, contributed to Southey's *Omniana*, Coleridge holds firmly to this point: the imagination, or 'shaping or modifying power', is not to be confused with the fancy, or 'aggregative and associative power'.[3]

Wordsworth disagreed. In *The Prelude* he uses the word 'fancy' rather casually about a dozen times (nearly twice as often in the 1850 text, where it usually gets a capital). Often it appears to mean simply the free play of mind. Occasionally (especially in 1850) it means the ability to form a picture in the mind, so that the word has much the same range of reference as the popular sense of 'imagination'. In Book VIII, however, Wordsworth distinguishes the wilfulness of fancy from the imagination's more serious work. To the examples he gives of that wilfulness (VIII.511–623) it may be worth adding, since it illustrates this point very clearly, one of his own shorter pieces. In the year 1802 he addressed three poems to the daisy. In the second of these, the one that begins 'With little here to do or see', Wordsworth's mind is evidently idling. The daisy, in the course of sixteen lines, becomes a nun demure of lowly port, a sprightly maiden of Love's court, a queen in crown of rubies drest, a little Cyclops with one eye, a silver shield with boss of gold, and so on. The link, if there is one, between these images, Wordsworth leaves us to guess. Each sounds wholly arbitrary; as a collection they add nothing to each other. This is Coleridge's 'aggregative and associative power' at work, or rather at play.

Wordsworth, however, never took so poor a view of fancy as Coleridge did. In 1815 he brought out the first collected edition of his poems, with a new Preface. In this edition Wordsworth arranged the poems, as he was to do in each successive edition, not chronologically but on a curious plan of his own. The poems are divided into groups: partly according to the faculty of mind which, Wordsworth feels, was dominant in their composition, partly according to the period of human life to which they refer. Thus we have Poems of the Imagination, Poems of the Fancy, Poems Founded on the Affections, Poems Referring to the Period of Childhood, and so on.

Obviously these categories cut across each other: a poem of the imagination might equally well be classified as a poem of the affections or a poem of childhood. Still, Wordsworth was attached to his arrangement. Several pages of his 1815 Preface are therefore devoted to fancy and the imagination.

Wordsworth begins his Preface by listing the powers requisite for the production of poetry. They include: '4thly, Imagination and Fancy – to modify, to create, and to associate.' Coleridge can hardly have been pleased to see Imagination in fourth place, after Observation and Description, Sensibility, and Reflection; still less to see it bracketed in this way with Fancy. Wordsworth, however, makes it plain that he regards fancy too as a creative faculty, and takes issue with Coleridge's distinction in the *Omniana* article of 1812: 'to aggregate and to associate', says Wordsworth, are just as much activities of the imagination as of the fancy. He then goes on to blur the issue by dragging in another phrase, 'to evoke and combine', from a dictionary of synonyms he has already rejected as inadequate.

Coleridge could not leave the matter there. Wordsworth, in his view, had clouded a distinction he had taken considerable pains to make clear. In *Biographia Literaria*, finished in September 1815 though not published till 1817, he denies Wordsworth's claim that the 'aggregative and associative power' belongs at all to the imagination, and he goes on in his next chapter (ch. XIII) to re-affirm his own distinction. First he separates the primary imagination (this is a new concept: 'the living power and prime agent of all human perception') from the secondary, or poetic. Imagination in this sense, the poetic imagination: 'dissolves, diffuses, dissipates, in order to recreate.' Dissipates what? The world as we know it, the familiar, too familiar, scene from which custom has 'dried up the sparkle and the dewdrops': the world with all its rigid bounding lines (the work of the primary imagination) between objects – between, say, a huge stone, a sea-beast, and an old man. The poetic imagination dissolves these divisions in order to recreate, from the energy of fresh experience, something that has its own internal unity.

The imagination, then, is essentially vital. Fancy, on the contrary, 'has no other counters to play with but fixities and definites'. Like memory, it relies on association to bring together objects which have only an accidental connection with each other, and far from unifying these objects into something coherent, leaves them as disparate as it found them. Since it cannot 'dissolve, diffuse, dissipate', neither can it create.

We might add, though Coleridge does not say this, that fancy, as it can only play with fixities and definites, will usually find expression in simile rather than metaphor. Shelley's 'To a Skylark' is a scatter of similes, and the most striking evidence of the fancy at work is obviously the Metaphysical conceit. (Milton, Coleridge, observes, 'had a highly *imaginative*, Cowley a very *fanciful* mind').[4]

Of course the imagination too, though metaphor is its element, will often delight in simile. In the 1815 Preface Wordsworth analyses his own great simile of the huge stone/ sea-beast/old man ('Resolution and Independence', stanza IX) to show how the imagination confers additional properties on an object, or abstracts and modifies properties already there. But by 1815 the sap had gone out of Wordsworth's poetry, and his critical writing has none of the force and freshness of the Preface to *Lyrical Ballads*. Even his account of the sea-beast simile gives the impression of something deliberately constructed, rather than, as it must have been, elaborated from a passionate intuition.

For Wordsworth, as for Coleridge, fancy implies a more conscious hunting of analogies. Fancy, therefore, often becomes capricious, even whimsical. Our adjective (fanciful) retains that sense. But for Coleridge, after about 1800, the two faculties are radically distinct, and the imagination alone is truly creative. For Wordsworth fancy too is a creative faculty, and imagination 'aggregates and associates' no less than fancy does.

The difference between Wordsworth's position and Coleridge's was perhaps more semantic than real. At any rate, it should not be pressed too far. For both poets the imagination is incomparably more valuable: more deeply felt, more serious, and more truthful. None of Wordsworth's greatest poems appears in the group which in 1815 (and subsequent editions) he called Poems of the Fancy. To the group Poems of the Imagination, on the other hand, he assigned 'Tintern Abbey', 'Resolution and Independence', 'To the Cuckoo', two of the Lucy poems ('Three years she grew', 'A slumber did my spirit seal'), and two splendid extracts from *The Prelude*: the Boy of Winander, and the Simplon Pass.

Notes

1. Nature and the One Life

1 The 1795 version is explicit:

> Thus *God* would be the universal Soul,
> Mechaniz'd matter as th'organic harps
> And each one's Tunes be that, which each calls I.
> (*Poetical Works*, ed. E. H. Coleridge, 1967, pp. 520–1)

2 See H. W. Piper, *The Active Universe*, 1962, chapters 1–3, and Jonathan Wordsworth, *The Music of Humanity*, 1969, pp. 184–201. Wordsworth's additions to *An Evening Walk* can be found in an Apparatus Criticus to the poem in the *Poetical Works*, ed. E. de Selincourt and H. Darbishire, 5 vols., 1940–49, vol. 1.

3 So much so that Wordsworth later altered the lines to read 'he fans my cheek' and 'the joy he brings'.

4 For a note on the composition of *The Prelude*, see Appendix I.

5 The 1799 text (Part I, lines 186–9) reads:

> Ye powers of earth, ye genii of the springs,
> And ye that have your voices in the clouds,
> And ye that are familiars of the lakes
> And of the standing pools, . . .

6 The Norton editors observe that capitalisation and punctuation in the MSS are haphazard. They therefore use their own judgement about punctuation and retain capitals only for 'God', 'Nature', and undoubted personifications (Norton *Prelude*, p. 511).

7 *Spectator* no. 571, 23 July 1714, quoted by de Selincourt in his note to *Prelude* II.263.

8 'To the Memory of Sir Isaac Newton', 1727, lines 142–3.

9 For a fuller treatment of Wordsworth's divided feelings for nature, see David Ferry, *The Limits of Mortality*, Middletown, Conn., 1959, and Geoffrey H. Hartman, *Wordsworth's Poetry: 1787–1814*, 1964. Both books give more weight than I should do to the mystical element in Wordsworth's poetry.

10 *The Story of My Heart*, 1883, ch. 1.

11 The textual history, which is complex, is summarised in *The
   Ruined Cottage and The Pedlar*, ed. James Butler, Cornell, 1979,
   which prints transcripts of the relevant MSS, and in Jonathan
   Wordsworth's critical study, *The Music of Humanity*, 1969, which
   includes a good text of both poems. At some time between
   February and December 1799 Dorothy transcribed 'The Ruined
   Cottage' as a poem of 538 lines, with the 'Pedlar' material (a
   fragment of 31 lines, plus a coherent text of 356 lines) as an
   addendum. This is the MS which Jonathan Wordsworth uses as
   his basic text and which I follow in the present book.
      Wordsworth never published either 'The Ruined Cottage' or
   'The Pedlar' separately, though he thought of doing so and
   returned to 'The Pedlar' frequently between December 1801 and
   March 1802. By the spring of 1804 he had reunited the two texts
   as a poem of nearly 900 lines. With additions and revisions, this
   appeared as Book I of *The Excursion* in 1814.
12 Later he lifted a few more lines from the Fragment for use in
   Prelude VII (722–30).
13 For a valuable discussion of Wordsworth and the One Life with
   special reference to 'The Pedlar', see Jonathan Wordsworth, *The
   Music of Humanity*, 1969, pp. 184–241.
14 Like most of 'The Pedlar', they ended up in Book I of *The
   Excursion* (lines 153–62, 198–213). There is an echo of the sunrise
   paragraph in *Prelude* IV.330–45.
15 At one stage in Wordsworth's assembling of Part II of the 1799
   Prelude an explicitly pantheistic passage of 16 lines followed the
   'sentiment of being' paragraph. It was to these pantheistic lines
   (*The Prelude, 1798–99*, ed. Stephen Parrish, Cornell, 1977, pp.
   206–9) that 'If this be error' originally referred.
      By 1850 even the claim that 'in all things / I saw one life and
   felt that it was joy' has been removed, its place being taken by
   the orthodox:

> Wonder not
> If high the transport, great the joy I felt,
> Communing in this sort through earth and heaven
> With every form of creature, as it looked
> Towards the Uncreated with a countenance
> Of adoration, with an eye of love.   (1850, II.409–14)

16 Again the pantheistic overtones are carefully qualified by 1850:

> O Soul of Nature! that, by laws divine
> Sustained and governed, still dost overflow
> With an impassioned life . . .   (1850, XII.102–4)

17 Most of 'The Pedlar' was incorporated in Book I of *The Excursion*
   (1814), and at the opening of Book IX of that poem the Wanderer

explicitly reaffirms that there is 'an *active* principle' which subsists

> In all things, in all natures; in the stars
> Of azure heaven, the unenduring clouds,
> In flower and tree, in every pebbly stone
> That paves the brooks, the stationary rocks,
> The moving waters, and the invisible air.

Significantly, though, the first version of these lines dates from the spring of 1798, when 'The Pedlar' was drafted.

2. The Mind and the World

1 *Spectator* no. 411, 21 June 1712.
2 For a detailed study of Wordsworth's awareness of the dilemmas of sense perception, see C. C. Clarke, *Romantic Paradox*, 1962.
3 Wordsworth is writing of his own experience. In the first draft (Norton *Prelude*, p. 492) he shifts half way through the passage from 'he' and 'him' to 'my call' and 'my skill', so that by the close the whole scene 'Would enter unawares into my mind'.
4 Fenwick note to the 'Immortality Ode'.
5 *Poetical Works*, ed. de Selincourt and Darbishire, vol. 1, p. 164.
6 *The Ruined Cottage and The Pedlar*, ed. James Butler, Cornell, 1979, pp. 468–75.
7 *Rasselas*, ch. 43.
8 *Modern Painters*, vol. III, Part 4, ch. 16.
9 For the pathetic fallacy, see Ruskin, *Modern Painters*, vol. III, Part 4, ch. 12; for the objective correlative, the essay on *Hamlet* in T. S. Eliot's *Selected Essays*, 1932.
10 For a good account of these early poems, see Paul D. Sheats, *The Making of Wordsworth's Poetry 1785–1798*, Harvard, 1973, chapters I and II, and F. W. Bateson, *Wordsworth: a Re-Interpretation*, 1954, ch. 2. Bateson (p. 186) suggests that the primary source of all Wordsworth's best poetry was his need to integrate the subjective and objective aspects of his personality.
11 D. H. Lawrence, 'Introduction to These Paintings', *Phoenix*, 1961, p. 559: 'the imagination is a kindled state of consciousness in which intuitive awareness predominates'.
12 *Scrutiny*, VII, 1 (1938), pp. 33–55; reprinted in *A Selection from Scrutiny*, 1968, vol. 2.
13 *Biographia Literaria*, ch. XIV.
14 Letter to Wordsworth, 30 May 1815, and *Table Talk* for 21 July 1832. Coleridge's own critique of Locke can be found as early as February 1801 in a series of four letters to Josiah Wedgwood.
15 See Appendix II.

3. Imagination

1 *Spectator*, no. 411, 21 June 1712.

2 *The Pleasures of the Imagination*, 1757, General Argument.

3 As above.

4 *The Pleasures of the Imagination*, IV.38–51.

5 A little joke of Valéry's, alluding to the opening of Virgil's first Eclogue: 'Tityrus, lying beneath the spreading shade of a beech tree, / You meditate the woodland muse.'

6 The Symbolists had little interest in Schopenhauer's concept of the will, which is central to his philosophy. What attracted them was his argument that each of us lives in a world of his own. See Rémy de Gourmont, preface to *Le Livre des Masques*, 1896, and A. G. Lehmann, *The Symbolist Aesthetic in France*, 1950, pp. 37–67.

7 Fenwick note to 'The Thorn'.

8 *Biographia Literaria*, ch. IV. The poem which so impressed Coleridge was the 'Adventures on Salisbury Plain', which Wordsworth later revised and published as 'Guilt and Sorrow'.

9 In his copy of Wordsworth Blake wrote in the margin, 'One power alone makes a poet: Imagination, the Divine Vision'. But Blake's mind was very different from Wordsworth's, and they did not mean the same thing by 'imagination'.

10 See Appendix II.

11 I am concerned only with the way the whole sequence is introduced, but it is also true, as Jonathan Wordsworth points out (Norton *Prelude*, pp. 568–70), that the poetry of the Penrith beacon episode (the woman with the pitcher) has been weakened between 1799 and 1805, as if Wordsworth was no longer in touch with his experience.

12 The lines that introduce the spots of time in 1850, though very close to the 1805 text, seem to recognise that the mind was not completely dominant in either episode:

> This efficacious spirit chiefly lurks
> Among those passages of life that give
> Profoundest knowledge to what point, and how,
> The mind is lord and master – outward sense
> The obedient servant of her will.   (1850, XII.219–23)

13 To be exact, the first nine lines of the meditation were composed in March 1804, when the spots of time were to bring the five-book *Prelude* to a close. The last six lines (XI.337–42) appear to be later, perhaps as late as April/May 1805. See Norton *Prelude*, pp. 516–17.

14 Norton *Prelude*, p.434, n.9. See Mary Moorman, *William Wordsworth: a Biography, the Later Years, 1803–1850*, 1965, pp. 1–2, 19–20, and Mark L. Reed, *Wordsworth: the Chronology of the Middle Years, 1800–1815*, Harvard, 1975, p. 247.

15 'To that dream-like vividness and splendour which invest objects of sight in childhood, everyone, I believe, if he would look back,

could bear testimony' (Fenwick note to the 'Immortality Ode').

16 See above, p. 40.

17 Plato's myth of the pre-existence of the soul, which gives Wordsworth his central metaphor in stanza V of the 'Ode', is tentatively endorsed in *The Prelude* as early as a passage composed in the winter of 1798/99 (I.580–5 of the 1805 *Prelude*). It turns up again in four passages of early 1804: III.178–81; V.531–6, 558–62; XI.229–32.

18 After their mother's death, when Wordsworth was eight, Dorothy lived for some years with a cousin of her mother's in Yorkshire, so that she and Wordsworth rarely saw each other.

19 In 'Michael' Wordsworth says that he was led to feel 'For passions that were not my own' by the stories he heard as a boy of shepherds like Michael, who had lived among the fields and hills which he (Wordsworth) knew and loved. Something of this comes through in *Prelude* VIII.211–311, but less clearly.

20 The text of the 1798 version of the Discharged Soldier can be found in *William Wordsworth (the Oxford Authors)*, ed. Stephen Gill, 1984, pp. 45–9.

21 *Prelude* VIII.211–15, 770–802; IX.481–503; X.290–305.

22 *Biographia Literaria*, ch. XXII.

23 *Table Talk*, 16 February 1833.

24 The 1850 text, though inferior as poetry, at least makes things a little clearer: the mist is now firmly subordinated to the moon (XIV.50–56) and the chasm no longer lodges 'the imagination of the whole'. Sacrificed here for the sake of intelligibility, the notion of the mind as an abyss is transferred to the crossing of the Alps (1850, VI.592–6). For a fuller discussion of the Snowdon sequence, see Jonathan Wordsworth, *William Wordsworth: The Borders of Vision*, 1982, ch. 10.

25 A first sketch for this image of a crag transformed by mist to an island appears at lines 5–18 of 'The Vale of Esthwaite', written when Wordsworth was seventeen (*Poetical Works*, vol. 1, p. 270).

26 *Prose Works of William Wordsworth*, ed. W. J. B. Owen and Jane W. Smyser, 3 vols., 1974, vol. II, p. 176.

27 *Prose Works*, vol. II, pp. 244, 369.

28 The Snowdon sequence, including the lines we are concerned with (XIII.102–5), was drafted in February 1804 when Wordsworth envisaged *The Prelude* as a poem in five books. In March he decided to enlarge his scheme. Book VI, with the crossing of the Alps and the 'unfathered vapour' paragraph, was composed in March/April 1804.

Appendix I: Composition of The Prelude

1 No MS of I.1–271 exists earlier than 1804. The likeliest dates of

composition seem to be November 1799 (for lines 1–54) and January/February 1804 (lines 55–271).
2 Possibly Wordsworth was already thinking of publishing these lines separately. They appeared in the second edition of *Lyrical Ballads* (1800).
3 A fragment, probably III.1–167, was composed in December 1801. An entry in Dorothy's Journal for 11 January 1803 records that 'in the morning William was working at his poem to C.' (i.e., *The Prelude*), but this may simply refer to some rewriting.

Appendix II: Imagination and Fancy

1 Johnson's second and third definitions of Imagination are:
    2. Conception; image in the mind; idea.
    3. Contrivance; scheme.
In chapter 32 of *Rasselas* (I owe this point to Moira Megaw) Imlac uses the word in a larger and more modern sense: the Great Pyramid, he observes, 'seems to have been erected only in compliance with that hunger of imagination which preys incessantly upon life, and must be always appeased by some employment'. Chapter 44, on the Dangerous Prevalence of Imagination, retains something of that larger sense, but twice switches to the word 'fancy' as if Johnson still habitually thought of the two terms as interchangeable.
2 *Biographia Literaria*, ch. IV.
3 Quoted by Coleridge, *Biographia Literaria*, ch. XII (final paragraph).
4 *Biographia Literaria*, ch. IV.

Index

The notes are not indexed.